NO LONGER PROPERTY OF
ANYTHINK LIBRARIES /
RANGEVIEW LIBRARY DISTRICT

grace like
Scarlett

grace like
Scarlett

GRIEVING WITH HOPE
AFTER MISCARRIAGE
AND LOSS

ADRIEL BOOKER

BakerBooks

a division of Baker Publishing Group
Grand Rapids, Michigan

© 2018 by Adriel McIntosh Booker

Published by Baker Books
a division of Baker Publishing Group
PO Box 6287, Grand Rapids, MI 49516-6287
www.bakerbooks.com

Printed in the United States of America

All rights reserved. No part of this publication may be reproduced, stored in a retrieval system, or transmitted in any form or by any means—for example, electronic, photocopy, recording—without the prior written permission of the publisher. The only exception is brief quotations in printed reviews.

Library of Congress Cataloging-in-Publication Data
Names: Booker, Adriel, 1977– author.
Title: Grace like Scarlett : grieving with hope after miscarriage and loss / Adriel Booker.
Description: Grand Rapids : Baker Publishing Group, 2018.
Identifiers: LCCN 2017053747 | ISBN 9780801075810 (pbk.)
Subjects: LCSH: Suffering—Religious aspects—Christianity. | Loss (Psychology)—Religious aspects—Christianity. | Grief—Religious aspects—Christianity. | Bereavement—Religious aspects—Christianity.
Classification: LCC BV4909 .B66 2018 | DDC 248.8/66—dc23
LC record available at https://lccn.loc.gov/2017053747

Unless otherwise indicated, scripture quotations are from the *Holy Bible*, New Living Translation, copyright © 1996, 2004, 2015 by Tyndale House Foundation. Used by permission of Tyndale House Publishers, Inc., Carol Stream, Illinois 60188. All rights reserved.

Scripture quotations labeled ESV are from The Holy Bible, English Standard Version® (ESV®), copyright © 2001 by Crossway, a publishing ministry of Good News Publishers. Used by permission. All rights reserved. ESV Text Edition: 2011

Scripture quotations labeled KJV are from the King James Version of the Bible.

Scripture quotations labeled MSG are from THE MESSAGE. Copyright © by Eugene H. Peterson 1993, 1994, 1995, 1996, 2000, 2001, 2002. Used by permission of NavPress. All rights reserved. Represented by Tyndale House Publishers, Inc.

Scripture quotations labeled RSV are from the Revised Standard Version of the Bible, copyright 1952 [2nd edition, 1971] by the Division of Christian Education of the National Council of the Churches of Christ in the United States of America. Used by permission. All rights reserved.

Author is represented by literary agent Jenni Burke of D.C. Jacobson & Associates, LLC, an Author Management Company. www.dcjacobson.com

The names and details of the people and situations described in this book have been changed or presented in composite form in order to ensure the privacy of the individuals involved.

18 19 20 21 22 23 24   7 6 5 4 3 2 1

In keeping with biblical principles of creation stewardship, Baker Publishing Group advocates the responsible use of our natural resources. As a member of the Green Press Initiative, our company uses recycled paper when possible. The text paper of this book is composed in part of post-consumer waste.

sits down knee-to-knee with the brokenhearted. See this work if ever you've needed someone to go with you, be with you, hold you . . . and give voice to your speechless, aching places. This book is blood, air, food, and friend."

Erika Morrison, author of *Bandersnatch: An Invitation to Explore Your Unconventional Soul*

"Raw, real, and emotionally honest. *Grace Like Scarlett* is for anyone dealing with the heartbreak of losing a child or the messy and untamable nature of grief. In the end, Adriel Booker's story and message are about the journey to hope and joy. She lifts the chin of the tearstained face heavenward with the reminder that Jesus is making all things new and that beauty will rise from ashes. There are few resources for individuals or churches that I have found to be this succinct and powerful—I wholeheartedly recommend it!"

Ken Wytsma, pastor and author of *The Myth of Equality* and *The Grand Paradox*

"Adriel Booker is an experienced and empathetic guide, leading us through the raw valleys of love and loss with a keen eye toward truth, hope, and the enduring compassion of Jesus. As she shares the depths of her own story, she unearths the beauty that is so often hiding in the most difficult seasons. Her book is a treasure for every person struggling to see Jesus in the shadows of sorrow."

Bo Stern, pastor and author of *Beautiful Battlefields*

"This is the book I wish I'd had to guide me through my miscarriage grief years ago. With beautifully redemptive storytelling, Adriel reminds women they are not alone in their boundless emotions, desperate questions, and deep, deep grief. *Grace Like Scarlett* gently invites each tender reader to grow through the pain and to find their hope and healing rooted in Christ."

Jess Wolstenholm, coauthor of The Pregnancy and Baby Companion books and founder of Gather & Grow

"Adriel Booker's *Grace Like Scarlett* is a raw and challenging look at the impact of miscarriages not only in the life of every woman who has undergone such tragedy but also in communities of faith who seek to care for those who have lost. As a pastor, I find this book offers hope to those in my congregation who have and will walk through this valley. Read it and be ready to give copies to all those who need the encouragement this book provides."

Steve Mickel, lead pastor of Westside Church, Bend, Oregon

"When I experienced the loss of a pregnancy I wanted two things in that place of pain. First, to know that I was not alone in it. Second, to believe there was hope. Adriel Booker offers both in *Grace Like Scarlett*. I wish I'd had this book years ago."

Holley Gerth, bestselling author of *Fiercehearted* and *What Your Heart Needs for the Hard Days*

"Adriel is one of the biggest-hearted people I know, and the purity of her conviction comes through with every word she writes. I know her story will touch the brokenhearted and stir the souls of those who need it most."

Tsh Oxenreider, author of *At Home in the World*

"This powerful book is more than a book. It's a permission slip to feel what you need to feel. I've walked with several friends through their own miscarriages, and I have always wished that there was more that I could offer, do, or say. *Grace Like Scarlett* is 'the more.' This book is a wise and compassionate companion for moms who are grieving the child they never got to hold."

Jennifer Dukes Lee, author of *The Happiness Dare* and *Love Idol*

"In *Grace Like Scarlett,* Adriel does the hard work of excavating her experience of excruciating loss. Her words keep perfect balance as they dance along edges—grief on one side, joy on the other—never falling into despair or the platitudes of easy faith. Unflinchingly honest, unquestionably authentic, and unashamedly human, *Grace Like Scarlett* is a must-read for anyone who has or will endure suffering—which is to say, all of us."

Seth Haines, author of *Coming Clean: A Story of Faith*

"My heart has long been crying out for a book like this, and *Grace Like Scarlet* is a beautiful answer to that prayer. Adriel Booker offers such clear, comforting, and compassionate words to the woman who is walking through deep loss. Not only will she find hope and consolation in these pages but it will feel like she's found an understanding friend. I highly recommend this powerful and practical resource for anyone who is experiencing the lonely grief of miscarriage."

Lisa Jacobson, Club31Women.com

"Adriel Booker is a midwife and a griefwalker. In *Grace Like Scarlett* she takes the reader's hand, walks into the womb of loss, and

To Jesus
Jesus, this book is for you—to expose your goodness.
Thank you for loving me into seeing it.
I still have so much to discover.

To Ryan
Ryan, your name belongs on the cover with mine.
Thank you for wading into the deep with me.
This is our astonishing and spectacular journey,
and it's only just begun.
I love you.

No matter how deep our darkness,
he is deeper still.

Corrie ten Boom

Contents

Contents

Foreword

*S*tanding at the lucky beginning of a long line to the only bathroom in a Tuscan monastery, I thought about what depth of discipline it must take these monks to share such a small space. If that one tiny stall didn't make the monks intimate friends, then I'm not sure what would. Adriel had already slipped into the restroom ahead of us; after all, she was pregnant and had the right-of-way. We were quiet in the sacred air, which hung with the exquisite fragrances of Italian cooking herbs, and that was all we needed to hear Adriel through the door. It was the angry moan of grief, so strong and familiar that another friend and I immediately burst through to where Adriel sat exposed in agony, and she leaned into our sides, and we saw the blood, and we said no words. We only groaned what sounds the Holy Spirit gave us.

It had only been eight years before that terrible, holy night that I had last doubled over a heating pad, two lost babies in a row. It was one of the most painful and isolating experiences of my life. To desperately want a baby only to discover that he or she had no heartbeat was like falling blind into a chasm of impossible desire. There was no way to fix it. There was only the presence of God in a way I had never experienced, and in time I became grateful for a present God while loathing that such pain exists in our world. When we stood with Adriel in that tiny washroom, I felt it all over again: loathing and grace, the presence of God coupled with a desire to smash down walls.

When we left for that amazing writer's retreat to Italy, I had no idea the connections we would make, how intimate we'd become with friends we'd never met. It was that one-stall-shared-monastery-restroom kind of bonding. My husband and I showed up worn thin in the grief that came from months in the hospital with one of our sons. We came to Italy ripped open and ready to receive healing. I can remember it was the shared sufferings that brought our group to such close soul proximity, the ability to discuss sobriety, death, and lost dreams. It was the freedom to envision and experience beauty again alongside this shared suffering that made us lifelong friends with Adriel.

I suspect this book will do that for you too. Maybe hearing words said out loud that we had only ever let thrash around in the desert places of our souls is part of our learning to take the hard, deep dive she mentions in these pages. Maybe this space of shared suffering is also the space we need to dream again.

As a minister, fellow mother, girlfriend, and sister, I can't count how many times I've been a doula to women as their babies were leaving their bodies, but this book has been a reminder that the grief of losing a pregnancy is not one that really ever leaves us. It becomes ever a part of us.

Grace Like Scarlett is a timeless book because that's how grief works. You're never really done with it or undone from it. It's a voice of recognition, and maybe the acknowledgment that you're relearning how to be yourself. It's a room of shared suffering where too many of us find ourselves, hurting but not without hope.

Adriel writes with the authority of one who has endured suffering. She is a gifted teacher and a brave leader into the darker realms of faith. As she discusses the transformation that grief brings into our lives, she also acknowledges and then shoos away blame, comparison, false guilt, shame, and isolation. Though it's been years since I've experienced miscarriage, this book helped me remember and even shined a light into other areas of suffering that I hardly know how to address.

Amber C. Haines, author of *Wild in the Hollow*
Fayetteville, Arkansas, 2018

Introduction

Dear Grieving Mom

aybe your grief is fresh and raw and you're still reeling from the suffocating blow of a recent miscarriage. Or maybe you've long ago buried a secret grief but something within is probing you to lean in closer to the pain once again. Let me be as straightforward as possible with you: I can't answer the cosmic "why" of your miscarriage, but I can validate and help you understand your pain and grief. I want to link my arm with yours in hope as we look together toward the day when Jesus makes all things new.

I discovered something in the early days after my first miscarriage, when grief came pounding with incredible force: If I didn't dive deep, the waves of grief would absolutely pummel me. In surfing, this is called a "duck dive." The apostle Paul calls it being "hidden with Christ."[1]

I call it survival.

As I began to practice my own deep dive after losing our daughter, Scarlett Grace, to miscarriage, I discovered this was actually more than survival. It was an invitation: Would I find Jesus in the deep?

It's normal to be filled with questions when experiencing personal trauma. *What have I done to deserve this? Is this my fault? Why would God let this happen? Is he punishing me for something? What if God isn't who I thought he was? How can I go on with life as I once knew it? Will I ever feel normal again? Is God—or his goodness—even real? What if my whole faith is a sham?*

Because the grief of miscarriage often goes unspoken, these types of questions can eat away at the soul and confidence of a woman as she tries to shoulder the burden of them in secret. We'll look at some of these hard questions together, but first I must tell you this: It might seem impossible, but you can do this. You can lose and grieve and hope. The power of grief can, and sometimes will, sweep us off our feet. But we can learn how to breathe under the deep. We may even learn to open our eyes there. We *can* grieve with hope. We may be brokenhearted or even crushed, but we will not be destroyed. We might even find that, in our weakness, we're stronger than we think.

Scarlett *can* lead to grace—a grace I would need as two more miscarriages followed my first.

My husband, Ryan, and I have six children, only three of whom share our dinner table. Motherhood has been a brilliant teacher, exposing the paradox contained within the experience of my grief: Suffering and joy can coexist.

I still have moments of sadness over my babies lost to miscarriage, but now I also have wonder. It was in my darkest days as a mother that I found my brightest hope in Jesus. And yes, I understand how terribly cliché this can sound when you're left stunned and broken by loss. But it's true. True doesn't mean easy, but I promise you: Love will lead you there, even through questions that seem insurmountable when your life is in shambles.

I remember the days of wanting to crawl into a cave, find a place to curl up there in the quiet, and never wake up. It wasn't that I *actually* wanted to die, it's just that I didn't know how to live under the weight of my sadness and collapsed expectations.

Out of nowhere, sorrow would hit me like a heat wave, pressing on my chest, leaving me desperate to peel off layers so I could find some relief. But even while experiencing intense loneliness, I also remember feeling the sweetness of God's presence in some of those shadowy hours. Something told me his quietness wasn't abandonment—it was companionship.

This isn't to say I could always *feel* his presence, or that I didn't long for something more tangible—a touch or a word (a billboard in flashing neon lights with a backdrop of double rainbows would have been nice). But even when I felt like I was groping in the dark, I somehow knew there was a God acquainted with pain who stayed with me in mine.

But maybe this hasn't been your experience at all. Maybe you've picked up this book wondering how it might help your soul rest after what feels like endless grief or a faith that never quite recovered. Maybe God seems absent or quiet. Or maybe, in haste, you downloaded the first book you found online because those words—"no heartbeat"—have just been uttered in your direction and you're looking for a lifeline. Maybe you're wondering if you'll ever feel close to God again or if your faith is even worth holding on to while you wait. Maybe you just want to know you're not alone.

I wish I could tell you unequivocally that you will "feel" Jesus near when you need him most, but I cannot. Who am I to presume my experience will translate into yours? I will not. And this, friend, is the truth of grief: It's wild. Grief does not follow a blueprint. It minds no flowchart. It doesn't tick off boxes, it will not be contained in your favorite list app, and it most certainly won't stay put on the calendar.

Grief is wild like the sea, but it doesn't need to destroy us. We can't conquer it, but we *can* navigate it, and we can find Jesus there too.

Dive in, friend. Come with me. Let's go deep.

Grace Like Scarlett will not help you solve the problem of why your baby died. It won't help you systematically piece together a theology to address all of the mysteries of faith. It's certainly not a handbook with three magic steps to healing. And it will not make false promises about what the shape of your family will someday look like. But what I *can* promise you is this: As we dive in to the goodness of Jesus, he longs to do a profound work within you, and he *will* hold you as he guides you through the wild waves.

When pain and suffering inevitably find us, Jesus calls us into the deep.

Every sentence I've written in this book has been preceded and followed by a prayer for you—mother who has miscarried—and for our sisters who grieve from similar, yet distinct, forms of loss. (Please note that I won't write specifically to the grief of stillbirth, infertility, abortion, molar pregnancy, neonatal loss, or the many other variations of pregnancy and infant loss, though I recognize there are many common threads to our grief, and I trust God to meet you right where you're at as you read.)

Together we'll explore the nature of grief and suffering, the human experience of community when it helps and when it hurts, the goodness of God and the promises we can hold to, and what it means to be reborn into our new selves, transformed by this experience of suffering and our revelation of hope. At the end of the book are meaty appendixes filled with practical resources for you, as well as a letter for grieving dads that my husband wrote. (We recognize there's a lack of support for fathers who've experienced this unique grief; you can find more resources for him in appendix F.)

The book is written to be read as a whole, with each chapter building on the next, and I hope you will sense companionship as we explore life after miscarriage together. Please read at your own pace. You may find some sections harder to read than others because of where you are in your grief journey, or because certain ideas or theologies are holding you together in your grief. If that's the case, then pause to process and digest before reading further or circle back around when you're ready to continue going deeper.

My prayer is that you hear your own story and grief experience woven throughout mine and that you would discover Jesus in these pages, find yourself within his care, and perhaps even discover the gift that your experience of loss can give way to. This is our collective story of the grace to be found as we dare to extend our trembling souls into the arena of hope.

Make no mistake, this book will include Jesus. It has to. He changes everything. Even if you're not sure what you think of God right now, I urge you to consider the possibility he offers.

May you grant yourself permission to feel, to wrestle, and to be fully awake to your suffering. May your soul be nurtured. May you take your time and breathe deeply. May you use your last bit of strength to dive below the surface when you see those wild waves approaching. Will you let your Scarlett—your own personal pain—be a gateway for God's grace?

> The thought of my suffering . . .
>> is bitter beyond words.
> I will never forget this awful time,
>> as I grieve over my loss.
> Yet I still dare to hope
>> when I remember this:
> The faithful love of the LORD never ends!
>> His mercies never cease.
> Great is his faithfulness;
>> his mercies begin afresh each morning.
> I say to myself, "The LORD is my inheritance;
>> therefore, I will hope in him!" (Lam. 3:19–24)

When you look toward the goodness of God, dear heart, I promise you'll see it. Let's look there together.

May all God's grace abound to you.

Love,

Adriel

Part I

Blindsided

PUMMELED BY
THE FORCE OF LOSS

one

Among the Fields of Gold

She always wanted to become a wife and a mother, so it shocked me when she announced she had entered the convent.

But then this friend from high school explained to me her revelation that all along her heart had yearned to be married to Christ and to mother the church; she only needed to discover what the depths of her soul were crying out for. It was clear to see how much she adored Jesus and loved her vocation. The habit she wore she likened to a wedding ring: an extravagant sign for the world to see exactly who she belonged to.

It sounded romantic and beautiful and fitting for a woman as faithful as her, and yet was hard to wrap my young Protestant mind around. In my early twenties myself, as she was, I longed to get married and have children. I found a vocation void of those things admirable but incomprehensible—equal parts mystery and practicality.

We lived on different continents and sporadically kept in touch through letters. I smiled when I received her notes signed, "May God bless you and Mary keep you, Sister Maximilian Marie." She was no longer my friend Loretta, yet was more herself than ever.

Now, both of us well into our thirties, I planned to visit her in Rome after attending a ten-day writing retreat in Tuscany.

The Eternal City

I landed in Rome excited to see my high school friend. We were twenty years removed from jazz choir and our after-school jobs at a nearby daycare center, but I had the excitement of a young freshman regardless. I was a Protestant pilgrim on my first visit to Vatican City, bursting with anticipation about learning church history and tradition and the sacraments through the Roman Catholic eyes of my devoted friend.

What I was *not* expecting during my brief two-day visit to Rome was that, after joining with the masses at Saint Peter's Square to hear the noonday Angelus prayer and blessing from Pope Francis, I'd be waving down a taxi knowing something was drastically wrong despite my very full heart.

The presence of blood is hard to deny.

Within the hour I was labeled "patient #788" in the emergency department of Gemelli Hospital while bleeding my dreams and my eleven-week-old baby down the toilet.

Perhaps that sounds coarse; it *should*, because it *was*.

Patient #788

Stuffed into a narrow hallway in the obstetrics area of the emergency department, I waited for my number to be called. All around me swollen bellies attached to hopeful mothers reminded me that I didn't belong to them anymore. I knew what was happening; this wasn't my first miscarriage.

"Drop your pants," the doctor instructed after leading me into the examination room and exchanging awkward hellos through her broken English (and my almost nonexistent Italian).

From the other side of the curtain I heard the loud *whoosh-whoosh-whoosh* of a baby's heartbeat on the fetal monitor. What was once a magnificent melody now taunted me—the rhythm of a slow, quiet torture I couldn't escape. I would have traded almost anything for a closed door, an ounce of privacy.

Deflated, I sunk onto the examination table and obediently spread-eagled, placing my feet in the halters. *Will I get kicked out if I throw my shoe at the whooshing machine across the room?* I can't remember feeling more humiliated. Ever.

Sister waited on the other side of the wall; I missed her and tried to visualize her there praying for me.

Our Father in heaven, hallowed be your name. Your kingdom come, your will be done, on earth as it is in heaven.[1]

The obstetrician scanned my uterus and I recognized the black, empty screen. I had seen it before—the kind of *nothing* that's enough to simultaneously set your eyes ablaze *and* extinguish the brightest hope. I hated that cursed technology—mocking my emptiness, leaving no room for possibility. Surely "nonviable" is among the most revolting terms a mother has ever heard.

I bled all over the examination paper and cringed when she removed it to reveal it had seeped through and now covered the table. In haste she poured half a bottle of disinfectant on the vinyl to rub off the excess "products of conception" that my body was rejecting. I felt both disgust and satisfaction that a stain seemed to remain.

Miscarriage is ugly.

It was irrelevant how much experience or logic was stored up in the files of my brain; in that moment I deemed myself an utter failure. My body was a tomb and I hated it.

The doctor pressed for details. *Was I certain I was pregnant? Could my estimation of dates be off?* The dead fetus measured weeks smaller than the eleven weeks I had professed.

"This was my fourth pregnancy. I may be sad but I'm not an idiot," I snapped. (Not my finest moment.)

Her English was better than my Italian, but it seemed there was an awful lot of guesswork as we each tried to determine what the other was saying. And was I even listening? *I'm not sure I was listening.* She was doing her job but all I could think was, *My God, why do my babies stop growing?*

I couldn't believe this was happening. Not here. Not now. Not again.

Maybe the only thing worse than carrying a dead baby is finding out you've been carrying a dead baby while blissfully unaware. I felt like a giant naive fraud of a mother who'd been prancing around gleefully pregnant while in actuality my body was a walking death sentence. The thought repulsed me.

When the examination was finished, I was told I'd need to wait three hours for my blood test results to come back so they could determine the best course of action. I asked to lie down and was put on a rollaway cot in the hallway. *In the hallway.*

Turning my back to the row of expectant mothers seated across from me—so close they were within arm's reach—I began to sob. I tried to hold it in; the last thing these hormonal, expecting women needed was a reason to be afraid or sad. (*Sad* seems such a grossly insufficient word here.) But there was no holding back the avalanche, and as soon as I started, a few of them followed suit. It was a symphony of my sobs and their sniffles, echoing around that otherwise quiet and still hallway.

These women knew precisely what was happening with the foreign girl curled up on the bed in front of them at exactly eye level. Maybe we were more alike than I thought.

It was in that moment I more fully understood Sister's vocation. Her hand rested gently on my back until my weeping slowed to whimpering. I was mothered by my friend who saw her very calling in life as a mother to God's people. Being separated from my family by an ocean was excruciating, but she cared for me and loved me as I needed in that desperate hour. She was Jesus in a habit, and I loved her something fierce.

But before Rome was Tuscany.

A Dream Called Tuscany

When we arrived at the luxury villa in Tuscany for our writers' retreat, we joked about stumbling into heaven on earth. Our villa overlooked the painted countryside, our towels came wrapped in satin ribbon tied into bows, and fresh pastries were delivered before dawn each morning. The view from my bedroom window boasted olive trees and honeybees going about the work of the centuries. We shared our thousand-year-old walled-in village with two hundred townsfolk who took pride in their slow pace and their windows lined in linen and doorposts adorned in flowers. Soaking in the scent of jasmine and lavender, we feasted our eyes on golden wheat fields hemmed in by rows of cypress trees and vineyards swelling with what would become the finest of wines.

It was breathtaking.

These were gifts of pleasure for no other reason than to usher in delight and remind us to *taste and see that the Lord is good.*[2] We meditated on the sacraments of beauty and community, creativity and vocation, eating four- and five-course meals and exploring masterpiece landscapes that seemed too serene to be real. And yet they *were* real—it all was.

Together we relaxed into the generosity of God as he invited us to go deeper, to see wider, to listen closer. Loosening our grip on feelings of unworthiness and embracing God's abundance became our work and our rest. You might think it all sounds terribly romantic, and you're exactly right. It was. It was a dream.

Under the Monastery Stairs

Toward the end of our retreat, we dined in a monastery, eating ourselves happy on another four-course meal. I left my wineglass untouched, ever attentive to the little one I carried. We swapped stories and shook our heads, recounting the ways Tuscany had swept us off our feet.

Before the drive back to our villa, I visited the restroom, and it was there I first saw the blood.

Tucked away in the tiny stall under the stairs where monks had once hushed their way to vespers and lonely rooms for solitary study and quiet communion with the God of hidden places, I ruptured the peace with groans and flailing. Within seconds, two of my brand-new friends were stuffed into the stall along with me while I wailed that I was having a miscarriage.

No, no, no, no, no. . . . I can't remember saying much of anything else. I wanted to rage against the darkness around me—that, I remember vividly. If I could have torn down those ancient stone walls or ripped the giant support beams out of the ceiling with my trembling fingers, I would have.

For the first time I understood the passages in the Old Testament that speak of mourners tearing their clothes and rubbing themselves in ashes—that sort of expression would have felt entirely appropriate as an external outworking of my internal anguish and lament. I distinctly remember wanting to tear my clothes off and throw myself into a fetal position on the floor.

After I had caught my breath and pulled myself together enough to stumble out from beneath the stairs, I stepped into the courtyard. I felt as if the canopy of lights in the night sky that had inspired artists for centuries now betrayed me. If only I could crawl under the dirt and hide from all that wretched beauty.

But I couldn't. So instead I blundered to the parking lot where the others were huddled, waiting and whispering, and then stood in disbelief as this tiny band of writers whom I had fallen in love with gathered around me and held me and prayed for me. I don't remember much from those moments, but I do remember one laying hands on my head and another praying to the God who holds all things together.[3]

Those writers lodged into my heart there under the wide Tuscan sky.

Is this God still holding me together? I wondered. I wanted to believe. But in that moment all I could do was breathe. Barely.

During the thirty-minute car ride, I tried to rationalize what was happening (*This is common, a little spotting is no big deal, it's the hormonal fluctuation as I change trimesters*), but I couldn't deny that for several days I had felt much more "normal" than I had before the trip. Where was the mild undercurrent of nausea? Where was the debilitating fatigue I had experienced for weeks? Why were my breasts no longer tender? Why did my fleshy belly feel less swollen and more "squishy" during the last few days?

The truth is, *I didn't want to know the answers to those questions.* If my worst fear was materializing, I wanted to deny it until I was home with my family. I wanted to stay in the Tuscan dreamland where everything hummed with the illusion of perfection.

But the other truth is, when you've lost a baby before, no amount of logic can shoo away the fear when the first sign of death creeps gingerly into your underpants. *This wasn't supposed to happen. Not like this. Not while I'm a world away from my family. Not during my Tuscan dream.*

The dream, it seemed, was hemorrhaging.

Suspended

When my Tuscan dream jolted into a full-scale nightmare in the hallway in Rome, I was confronted with another reality: I really hadn't found "heaven on earth" in Italy. No matter how wonderful our surroundings, no matter how perfect it all seems, we will never know and experience the fullness of heaven on earth until Jesus himself makes all things new. All that we see and taste and touch, though being redeemed, is still flawed—deeply and desperately.

The heartbreak and horror of what we experience in hospital waiting rooms and in our driveways and through our evening news and in Tuscany under a stairwell is part of this sacred reminder: Things are not as they should be, *but they will be.*

Jesus is making all things new. Heaven is at hand and heaven is still coming.

I wanted to linger in the romance, believing perfection was within my reach. But seeing the lifeless ultrasound screen was a stark reminder that we still live in the tension between the *now* and the *not yet.* Jesus has come but he is still coming. Restoration has drawn near but it's still approaching. Heaven is at hand but it's still descending. Every tear will be wiped away but for now we still have reason to cry.

My Sunday in Gemelli Hospital left me suspended—neither pregnant nor unpregnant—with a day of limbo before my flight home. I rejected the offer of a D&C (surgical removal of the baby) and decided instead to try my luck at getting back to Ryan and finishing the miscarriage naturally. Although I had chosen a D&C after my first miscarriage, I wasn't keen on surgery in a foreign country where my lack of language left more guesswork than I was comfortable with.

I spent Monday trying my best to blend in with the throngs of tourists in Rome. The best thing I could do for myself, given the circumstances, was to try to make the most of my last day in Italy. I couldn't exactly pretend as if nothing was wrong, but I couldn't pretend nothing was right, either. It felt ridiculous and desperate, simultaneously fraudulent and authentic.

Rome is truly enchanting; she made space for my pain in the midst of exquisite beauty. I marveled at the wonders of Saint Peter's Basilica and the Sistine Chapel—surrounded by manmade creation (clearly inspired by the Creator) while carrying death in my belly. I cried before Michelangelo's sculpture of the Virgin Mother weeping and cradling her lifeless son. I offered tears as prayers when the words wouldn't come. The significance and the irony of holding life and death and the hope of resurrection within me while in the Eternal City wasn't lost on me.

The next morning I packed up the jumbled mess of my Italy experience and boarded a plane back to America. I was a hurricane of emotions in search of a shore that would tame and downgrade the storm and untangle the currents pulling me in opposing directions. How could one experience contain such soaring heights and crushing lows? It was all so confusing. I needed the concrete reassurance my husband's arms could give me.

Delivering Death

Almost exactly twenty-four hours after landing in Oregon, I labored and birthed our lifeless child.

The process sideswiped me, each contraction inviting the rush of pain and injustice and agony all over again. I had no idea this concoction of physical and emotional pain was possible; somewhere I had picked up the notion that a natural miscarriage would feel more *natural*. I was wrong. *This whole thing was wrong.* A mother shouldn't have to say goodbye to her child. It feels unnatural because it *is*.

I rocked through each contraction, wailing in pain and wishing someone could put me out of my anguish and wake me up when it was all over. Laboring was a misery unparalleled. Unaccompanied by the endorphins, adrenaline, and promise of holding a child on the other side of the pain, I felt each wave of cramping like another slap in the face—layers of pain, compounding.

Thoughts of laboring a dead baby spun in my mind, and I wished I could take those hours back in Rome and readmit myself to the hospital for the D&C like the doctor had recommended. I realize every woman handles this sort of thing differently—and for some, miscarrying naturally resembles a heavy period—but not for me. This was full-blown labor, with no midwife there to cheer me on. I loathed every second of it and longed for the familiarity of waking up from the anesthesia with someone whispering, "Don't worry, it's all over now." At least when they scraped our first miscarried child from my womb I could blame the doctors for taking her. This time I couldn't shift that awful burden to anyone else; I was the one who delivered this child to his grave.

My doctor later explained to me that not every miscarriage ends with such physical pain, but that experiencing harsh contractions is not uncommon either. She apologized for not having had the opportunity to give me adequate pain relief before the onset of labor, and for not more thoroughly briefing me over the phone when I called, desperate, from Italy. (Our distance understandably brought limitations.)

Even though I had experienced twenty-one hours of painful back labor with no medication during our son Judah's birth, I was not prepared for the intensity of this pain. The physical pain was awful; the emotional pain was worse. Losing one child felt like a tragedy that happened *to* me. Losing a second felt like something happened *through* me and because of me.

In the aftermath of this second miscarriage, I was a furnace of anger, yet over and again God entered my flames, offering peace for my chaos, hope for my grief.

Peace, Beloved

We named our baby Oliver David. *Oliver* means "peace," which we sensed God extending to us in the trauma that felt like war on our souls. *David* means "beloved."

These names represented God's heart and promise for us, and I believe they are a twofold promise for you too: Jesus offers peace when everything else feels upside down, inside out, and on fire. And *you* are beloved, no matter how broken you feel.

two

Hello, Deep Dive

*I*t's said that having children is like having your heart walk around outside of your body. If that's true, it's no wonder miscarriage feels like having part of your heart missing.

My heart has been exposed to this phenomenon for over seven years now. First with the birth of two sons. Then with the trauma of three miscarriages. And then again during the physically difficult and emotionally fraught pregnancy and delivery of our youngest son. Six pregnancies to practice the deep dive. I'm still learning how to go deep enough.

When I became pregnant for the first time, my heart came alive with possibility. I loved being with child and was proud of my growing belly. I was healthy, happy, active, and full of expectation. I treasured pregnancy as the only time I wouldn't have to share my little one with the world and enjoyed rearranging my life around this tiny growing piece of my heart. Motherhood was changing me already; it felt good and right.

Levi was born after twelve hours of labor and a swift emergency cesarean section. He was perfect and I was drunk on love.

Although the hardest, most exhausting work of my life, mother-hood was everything I'd hoped for. My heart was ablaze. I was born for this.

A year later we conceived our next child, Judah, as soon as we began trying. Amazing. We were delighted to add to our family, and thankful it was happening so easily.

This was also the pregnancy where I first learned to deep dive.

Initiation into the Waves

For couples who choose to do so, one of the most thrilling moments in a normal pregnancy is finding out the gender of the baby during the mid-pregnancy morphology scan, but we knew something was wrong when the ultrasound technician rotated out for a more experienced sonographer, who then changed places with a doctor. We were stunned when a specialist pulled us into his office after the scan and began speaking about our baby boy in a foreign language: *Trisomy 18, Trisomy 13, "incompatible with life," Trisomy 21.*

Our baby had several markers that pointed to a chromosomal anomaly, but we couldn't be certain without further testing. The specialist explained our options, and we left nauseated by the thought of our child dying in utero, or the alternative he was gently offering.

We left the hospital that day in a blur, begging God for the least severe option—Down syndrome—which the specialist said was our "best-case scenario."

Devastation flattened us.

Against doctor's orders, I googled way too much. I also asked friends and family to pray. I journaled. I poured out my grief and fear before the Lord. I cried. I blubbered and snotted. (A lot.) The thought of losing a baby horrified me.

A few days later we had a follow-up visit with another doctor. We entered nervously, desperately hoping for any news that might suggest there was hope for our baby's life. As she unpacked the reports and stats and medical jargon, she clarified that the previous doctor had misled us. In fact, the chances of our baby having a life-threatening anomaly (such as Trisomy 13 or 18) were extremely low, and it was much more likely he'd be born with Down syndrome (Trisomy 21). Her assessment, though still difficult, was an enormous relief. We left thankful and weepy.

Through the anguish of the *not knowing* and the powerlessness we felt over our circumstances, we began to learn what grief and suffering can do to a human soul—it stretches it wide open to fit all of the anguish and confusion and sorrow and humanity that's exposed. We had to dive deep in order to not be destroyed. And we did so, together.

Perfecting the Duck Dive

Surfers learn early on that unless they want to get swept back to shore, they have to learn to duck dive—take the whole surfboard and duck underneath the coming wave. Instead of trying to get over it or around it, they know the best way through is to go under. If they don't duck dive properly, they'll get pummeled.

I've been surfing a few times. I wish I could tell you I'm a surfer, but I'm not. My first day surfing was on a giant longboard off the coast of San Diego, California, when I was sixteen or seventeen years old. I understood the weight distribution from my days of snowboarding powder where I grew up in Oregon; this was just warmer and wetter, right?

The waves were small and consistent—perfect for a beginner—and my borrowed board was gigantic, making it almost impossible *not* to get up. (Honestly, it was probably more like sailing than surfing.) The only problem was, I couldn't get out far enough to *catch* a wave; I simply couldn't get past the break. I understood the *concept* of duck diving, but I had no actual experience. I didn't have the technique, and I certainly didn't have the muscle to sink that bus of a surfboard under the ocean's surface.

After what felt like forever of paddling, paddling, heaving, and paddling some more, my friend finally told me to grab onto his ankle so he could pull me far enough out. He swapped my longboard for his shorty, and when it was time, I let go of his ankle and tried duck diving again. That time, I made it through in one piece, and, much to my delight, I was still moving forward. (And yes, I caught my first wave soon after!)

Here's what I learned about duck diving from the few surf sessions of my youth:

- You must have forward momentum when you're diving. You can't be stagnant and then expect to duck dive successfully. You've got to paddle as much as you're able until the last moment before diving.
- Just before the wave comes, you need to take a big breath. I guess this one's pretty self-explanatory, but it's amazing how we can sometimes forget to breathe, even—*especially*—when it's most important.
- As you dive, you lead with your hands, then your head, then your shoulders, and the rest of your body follows.
- Push down with your knee as much as you can and then lay flat on your board once you're under. If you've nailed the technique, you'll naturally emerge on the other side of the wave—not only having survived it but having moved forward.

Why all this talk about surfing? Because this duck dive became an important metaphor for me as I learned to navigate the waves of grief that started with Judah's prognosis and continued through the miscarriages that followed. I had to find Jesus underneath the surface.

Before our lives were interrupted with grief, my relationship with Jesus was good, *rich* even. To stick with the surfing analogy for a moment, you could say I wasn't a novice and yet had never faced big surf either.

I was practiced at spiritual duck diving—I knew my life needed forward momentum and that I'd drown without filling my lungs with God's presence. I also knew that at times my head and my heart didn't *feel* like connecting to Jesus, but if I just reached out my hands a little, my head and heart would follow. I also knew that once I was under the surface I could stretch out and trust the process, relaxing into the confidence that I would emerge on the other side.

But even though I knew how to go deep, my version of deep was about to be schooled. I needed to go way deeper; the break on the horizon was massive and I was on a heavy longboard.

The Faintest *Yes*

Here's where we have to deviate from the duck dive analogy for a moment. The reason is simple: When we are grieving, we don't need spiritual muscle to dive deep into Jesus. It helps if we've already developed muscle memory before being dropped into the North Shore, sure, but the grace of God means he isn't dependent on our strength, stamina, and precision.

All it takes is our slightest desire, our faintest *yes*, and he draws us under. I suppose we've got to want to dive, but he meets us in the surrender—our weakness releases his strength. His might is manifest in our dependence. People have a remarkable ability to endure hardship when they tap in to their inner strength, but when the source of your inner strength comes from something—*Someone*—greater than yourself, the reservoir is more vast than you dared imagine.

You'll find this as you grieve: Some days you'll have the strength to dive deep—and Jesus will meet you there. Other days you'll barely manage a nudge in his direction—and he'll meet you there too. His grace is big enough for both.

Under the Deep

As Ryan and I digested the prognosis for our son, the waves of fear and sorrow and grief came with crushing intensity—powerful and close together—but we learned to fill our lungs and dive deep into the safety of Jesus. We had no assurance for Judah's life or health, but we did have God's promise to stay with us under the waves.

We were on the edge of transformation, and we could feel it.

Grief invites us to a liminal space—a place to hold on to the comfort and presence of God while suspended between who you are and who you're becoming. Liminal spaces feel disorienting because they are.

The word *liminal* comes from the Latin word *limina* or *limen* and connotes the idea of a threshold—a space between what was and what will be. The implication is a *moving forward* into something new, but not without first being transformed by the in-between.

Liminal spaces demand our attention, not just as a means to an end but as a place of transformation. Richard Rohr describes a liminal space as being "in between your old comfort zone and any possible new answer," and likens it to "Israel in the desert, Joseph in the pit, Jonah in the belly, the three Marys tending to the tomb."[1]

"This is the sacred space where the old world is able to fall apart, and a bigger world is revealed," Rohr says. It's the "threshold of God's waiting room."[2]

It did seem as if our old world was falling apart, but we were only beginning to catch glimpses of the new one. We felt the movements toward a certain kind of coming of age of our faith—realizing that God's goodness was not dependent on our assessment of our circumstances or the metrics we tend to use when life is comfortable. (I don't know about you, but we are sometimes guilty of enjoying favorable circumstances or breakthroughs and proclaiming, "Isn't

God good?!" while conveniently forgetting to proclaim his goodness when life unfolds in ways that hurt.)

While this belief about God's goodness through all of life's circumstances wasn't new to us, the depth of understanding was. It was like learning to open your eyes under water: Even though you know it's possible, it feels awkward, frightening, and cumbersome at first. And yet the more you practice, the more natural and liberating it feels. Eyes wide open to God's goodness—*especially* when it feels risky—changes the way everything else looks too.

Deeper, Still

We learned about Down syndrome in measured doses as Judah's birth approached, attempting to cushion ourselves from overload or obsessing about what was still unconfirmed. I imagined myself as a mom of a child with special needs, and my thoughts slowly shifted from how it might affect our child and family negatively to how it might transform and enrich our lives as we learned to be changed by this little boy. We moved toward birth with expectancy and peace.

And then he came.

A week before his due date I pulled our gorgeous son to my chest in adrenaline-soaked euphoria after an arduous twenty-one-hour labor. It wasn't until fifteen minutes later, when my brain caught up to my heart, that I realized he had been born without Down syndrome.

All of that. For what?

Those pregnant days of holding space for both grief and hope shaped us in ways as a couple and as parents that would become an anchor in the days to come.

We learned to dive deep into Jesus, and even open our eyes under the water, but we would need to go deeper, still.

Part I
Invitation

Journal Prompt: Before moving on to part II, write out your own personal story of loss. Include as much detail as you can recall about what happened and how you felt. Don't worry about your writing skills or stop to edit; this is to help you remember, and you don't need to share it with anyone right now. Try to resist writing about lessons you learned or sermonizing to yourself with things you think you "should" write. Let this simply be an exercise in telling your story.

Part II

Overboard

**WHEN YOU THINK
YOU MIGHT DROWN**

three

The Spectacle of Heaven

Do you remember the feeling of your skin or the color of the walls or the sound of your gasp the moment the bottom first dropped out?

For me it was an ordinary Wednesday afternoon in April inside a tiny, windowless room where a still, black screen confronted us. It should have been alight with the fluttering heart of our thirteen-week-old baby girl. But it wasn't. It was silent.

I had experienced anguish after Judah's prognosis, yes, but his heart was still beating. We had hope for his life.

This was different. *This* screen left us with nothing.

Scarlett was dead, our first miscarriage.

While curled up on the bottom of our shower that night, choking on my own snot, I felt no more equipped to live or die than the refugees of war spread across the evening news. *How does one survive this terror?* Suffering is the great equalizer. *So this is what a broken heart feels like?* I became kindred to a hurting world that day. *Am I dying too?*

The pain of losing a child starts by breaking your heart and then courses through every single vein and vessel, consuming your body until your bones ache.

All of the events that would make up the next few days are mere details: the newborn's cry echoing in the hospital hallway while I waited for my D&C, the argument over gender testing with the insensitive surgeon, the dollar store dolphin print hanging crookedly above the examination bed, the nurse with the kind eyes who loved me, the way my husband looked like Jesus and reminded me I was not alone, the statistics and charts and pumping of needles, the shuffling in and out of clinics, the homemade cookies on my doorstep, the words spilling from my fingers, the whisper from heaven shattered around my feet, the image of Jesus carrying me in my exhaustion. These were trivialities propped up like matchsticks on my mountain of grief, folding together to make a story I hated—a story bearing my name.

How does a mother learn to breathe again after her baby dies? One breath in. One breath out. And then again. And again.

Suffering does not choose the weak or the strong, the faithful or the faithless. It chooses the *human*. When you are caught by waves that are larger than your capacity to stay above the surface, you've got to allow your heart to feel the pain all the way down to the bottom, so that when you get there you can see you're still alive. There's still hope. It's from the bottom that we can begin to heal our way back up to the surface. The human heart is fragile, yes, but it's also more resilient than we give ourselves credit for.

The deep is not our enemy or a thing to be resisted. But it does command our attention. No matter what form it takes, suffering *always* commands our attention. It will not be alleviated by comparison to greater or lesser suffering, or even your perception of it. Your pain is your pain and it deserves the dignity of recognition, for that is where healing begins.

44

Misery's Shadow

My most recent pregnancy resulted in the birth of a healthy son, Micah. He was born full-term and a million pounds strong. (Perhaps not a million, but nearly ten, which is basically the same thing.) In addition to the concoction of joy, anxiety, and fear of being pregnant after recurrent miscarriages, I also experienced debilitating physical pain all throughout the pregnancy. In layman's terms, my pelvis was falling apart. It felt like my whole body was coming unhinged.

I couldn't walk. I couldn't sleep. I couldn't climb stairs. I couldn't sit on the floor with my children or sit on the couch among friends. I couldn't push a loaded grocery cart. I couldn't clean. I couldn't take walks around our new neighborhood that I yearned to explore. Even with physiotherapy and braces, exercises and stretching, the pain was relentless.

In a season where I wanted to enjoy a pregnancy progressing as it should after three heartbreaking losses, I felt crushed under the suffering I experienced in my physical body. All the very worst news stories about planes plummeting through the sky or the Ebola epidemic ripping through Africa didn't cancel out what I endured within my own body and soul. I was suffering, and in my worst moments, all I could think about was my pain.

C. S. Lewis put it this way: "Part of every misery is, so to speak, the misery's shadow or reflection: the fact that you don't merely suffer but have to keep on thinking about the fact that you suffer."[1]

I struggled with a false sense of guilt, feeling resistant to naming my suffering for what it was. How could I call this "suffering" after having three miscarriages? What right had I to name this "suffering" when barren women would give anything to trade places with me?

Naming our suffering does not mean becoming defined by it. Rather, it means honestly acknowledging our need in the presence of Jesus. Our humility frees us to receive his grace. It's his beauty for our ashes—the great exchange, God's answer to our pain.

Our present suffering is the best reminder that life dishes out more than we can handle, which is exactly why we need Jesus.

Thy Will Be Done

When Jesus showed us how to pray, he acknowledged within his prayer that God's will is not always done on earth, yet we're to pray it *will* be.

Babies die before they're born. People are exploited for sex, power, and money. Violence ravages communities. Prisoners are beaten and tortured. Nations turn a blind eye to genocide happening next door. Racism kills dreams and claims lives. Abuse destroys families. Ego corrupts governments. Carelessness and apathy wreck oceans and forests. Disease steals children from their mamas and daddies.

We can watch the news and see that God's will isn't always happening; it seems obvious that monstrosities like the horror of war don't represent God's heart or intention. But what about when it's our life, our baby? Do we believe it then? Do we believe Jesus's prayer is still relevant? *Your kingdom come, your will be done, on earth as it is in heaven.*

We suffer because we live in a world where things are not as they should be. This is not God's design; we weren't created to suffer. The human story begins in Genesis chapter 1, not chapter 3.

Suffering exists, but not because it's God's intention or will for our lives. It exists because he created us with the capacity to love, and love always requires free will—it cannot be forced. With humanity's free will came the wonderful, awful ability to rebel against Love. Our rebellion in the garden set the world in motion toward suffering, and it still spins today, leaving brokenness in its wake.

This was not God's will then, and it's not God's will now.

All these years after Eden, we're still groaning under the weight of sorrow. Jesus has come, but we're still waiting for him to come again. He's saved us from ourselves, and he's still saving us as we awaken to his purposes and movement in our lives. The kingdom of God is at hand, and every day it's further established as we live *into* it and allow God to heal us and heal creation through us.

Our *in between* remains a tension. We hold the promise of hope and redemption in one hand and the reality of a world still infected with rebellion in the other. This is the reason "bad things happen to good people." This is the reason we continue to pray, *Your kingdom come, your will be done, on earth as it is in heaven.*

Lament as an Offering

While mourning the loss of Scarlett, I had to learn the song of lament. It was new to me, awkward and unfamiliar. I grew up singing about how awesome God is and how my soul longeth after him and how Jesus shines, but giving voice to anguish and the injustice of loss and brokenness, acknowledging the pain closing in around me—this I had to learn in the dark, arms open, tripping my way forward.

Lament is more than just sadness; lament acknowledges injustice mixed into our pain. Jemar Tisby describes it as "anguish out loud," and says it "communicates more than despair; it cries out for deliverance."[2]

> Save me, O God,
>   for the floodwaters are up to my neck.
> Deeper and deeper I sink into the mire;
>   I can't find a foothold.
> I am in deep water,
>   and the floods overwhelm me.
> I am exhausted from crying for help;
>   my throat is parched.
> My eyes are swollen with weeping,
>   waiting for my God to help me.

47

Those who hate me without cause
   outnumber the hairs on my head.
Many enemies try to destroy me with lies,
   demanding that I give back what I didn't steal.
     (Ps. 69:1–4)

O Lord, how long will you forget me? Forever?
   How long will you look the other way?
How long must I struggle with anguish in my soul,
   with sorrow in my heart every day?
How long will my enemy have the upper hand?
Turn and answer me, O Lord my God!
   Restore the sparkle to my eyes, or I will die. (13:1–3)

Almost half of the psalms are dedicated to lament—both corporate and personal—and yet it's all but absent from our tidy Sunday morning hymnals.[3] We're far more comfortable celebrating Jesus's victory than we are holding space for the reason we need it in the first place. And so, when suffering comes like a wrecking ball into our cozy status quo—as it does—we are blindsided.

When a mother is told her baby is growing in her fallopian tube and must be removed to save her life, she is blindsided. *Is this abortion?* she wonders, even though the doctor assures her the removal of an ectopic pregnancy and an abortion aren't the same thing.

When a couple has emptied their life savings to undergo fertility treatment and IVF only to receive the word "nonviable" from the other end of a phone call, they are blindsided. This felt like their last chance.

When a mother holds a newborn in her arms and calls her by name only to have the birth mother change her mind just before signing the adoption papers, she is blindsided. This, too, is a grief inexplicable.

When a couple watches their child play alone while month after month and year after year the calendar turns with no pink lines appearing, they are blindsided in slow motion. This mother would give the world to trade her tear-stained pillow for sleepless nights, pacing the floor with a newborn. This is hope deferred, making her heartsick.

How do we give language to this agony? What words do we use to cry out for deliverance from this pain?

Nothing I've experienced has made me more desperate for the hope of kingdom come than straddling a toilet, bleeding life from my womb. Nothing else has made me beg for God's deliverance, his day of reckoning, when every tear will be wiped away.

I never knew I could cry so much. Or hope so much.

Lament—it's the language of grief tinged with the hope for deliverance.

Grace like Scarlett

We named the daughter I miscarried Scarlett Grace. *Scarlett* was for the pain, the suffering, the life poured out mingled with the hope of resurrection. *Grace* was for possibility and purpose, goodness and life—the breathtaking assurance that God can be found in our suffering. God's promise to us is not that bad things won't happen, it's that he's with us through it all—Emmanuel, *God with us.*

We were beginning to see it.

The ache we endured after losing Scarlett helped uncover holes in our theology—chiefly, that we did not have a theology of suffering. A theology of suffering does not mean God *wills* it or leads us into it. It means that when suffering comes into our still-broken world—as it *will*—he can be found there too. Theoretically we understood this, but our bewilderment in the face of bottomless pain confirmed our lack of praxis. Simply put, we weren't living what we believed because we'd never had the chance to.

Although we felt sure God wasn't the *source* of our suffering, Ryan and I were only beginning to learn that the very thing the enemy of our souls used against us could be transformed by the redemptive hand of God.[4] This wonder-working God was in the process of transfiguring our horrible loss into an invitation to greater life. We couldn't discern it yet, but God was hovering, preparing to create something new like he always does when all we see is dark, formless, and void.[5]

Scarlett was taking us deeper. But to go there we had to be willing to disarm our knee-jerk instinct to distract, numb, or overcome our pain. We had to resist the impulse to deflect our grief or fight our brokenness. We had to reject the compulsion to figure out how this could be rewritten into a success story. We had to enter in *as is*.

The Low Places

The spectacle of heaven is that it's birthed into the low places. It's revealed when Jesus is allowed to enter into the lives of those who *know* their need for him: a woman caught in adultery, a fraud and a cheat, a hotheaded loudmouth, a terrorist, a thief, a desperate man and his son, a diseased outcast[6] . . . a mother staring at an empty ultrasound screen. Heaven is not merely a destination; it's the Spirit of God writing a redemption story right here and now among our brokenness.

We can get so busy dotting all the i's and crossing all the t's and making sure all the hatches are battened down that we don't even realize our need for God until something turns the world upside down. Trauma can be the birthplace of revelation if we're willing to be exposed to our need and welcome Jesus there.

But it's hard to be needy, isn't it, friend? Aren't we so much more comfortable being the *helper* than the *helped*? We'd rather be the ones lowering our friend through the roof to Jesus than being so broken we've got to be carried there by others.[7]

Choosing to walk in the way of vulnerability before Jesus and before others takes a certain kind of resolve. It requires tapping into a different place than where we store our ability to grit our teeth and sidestep pain. It looks less like scaling a mountain and more like crawling to an altar—laying ourselves bare before Jesus, weapons and defenses dropped, pride abandoned, hearts wide open asking for deliverance.

He sees our need and names it *Beautiful*, and we've never felt more loved in our life.

> Can anything ever separate us from Christ's love? Does it mean he no longer loves us if we have trouble or calamity, or are persecuted, or hungry, or destitute, or in danger, or threatened with death? . . . No, despite all these things, overwhelming victory is ours through Christ, who loved us.
>
> And I am convinced that nothing can ever separate us from God's love. Neither death nor life, neither angels nor demons, neither our fears for today nor our worries about tomorrow—*not even the powers of hell* can separate us from God's love. No power in the sky above or in the earth below—indeed, nothing in all creation will ever be able to separate us from the love of God that is revealed in Christ Jesus our Lord. (Rom. 8:35, 37–39, emphasis mine)

In the face of our suffering, Jesus stretches out his hand. Will we accept the invitation to dive deep *under* the waves rather than try to tame or outrun them? Will we understand that we are still loved?

> Come boldly to the throne of our gracious God. There we will receive his mercy, and we will find grace to help us when we need it most. (Heb. 4:16)

four

From the Dust

God enters into our suffering to blaze a redemption path out. But it still hurts. Suffering always hurts.

Sometimes suffering hurts like the word *nonviable* ricocheting with violence around the inside of an examination room, or the eruption of wailing that comes after.

Sometimes suffering hurts like applying lipstick and waterproof mascara before walking up the steps to a baby shower so you can fake-smile your way through "guess the baby food" with other grown women, eating puréed peas from tiny jars like it's no big deal.

Sometimes suffering hurts like crying through the worship set at church or packing up the baby clothes you had so carefully washed and folded.

Sometimes suffering hurts like celebrating someone else's miracle while resisting the urge to covet it as your own.

Sometimes suffering hurts loudly: sobbing and snotting in the back of a Target parking lot. And sometimes suffering hurts silently: heavy, empty arms and phantom kicks under the cover of nighttime.

Sometimes suffering hurts like aborted dreams—you weren't just expecting a baby, you were expecting forever.

The world is not yet as it should be.

He Sees. He Hears.

In Genesis 16 we see the messy story of two women caught in the crossfire of infertility and grief. Sarai, married to Abram (whom we'll later know as Sarah and Abraham), is unable to have a child. As was common practice during the time of the patriarchs, Sarai gave her servant Hagar to Abram in order that he may have a child and heir through her. When Hagar got pregnant, she became smug, spurring Sarai to burn with jealousy and lash out in abuse.

Hagar fled, finding herself alone, despised, and desperate. We can only imagine what she must have felt as she huddled in the dirt: What had she done to deserve this maltreatment? Wasn't this whole situation grossly out of her control? Was she not justified after being forced to make her womb available for someone else's husband?

This thing—this *baby*—she thought to be a blessing now felt like a curse as her life lay in shambles.

Then an angel of God breaks through her anguish, delivering a promise: God has seen her heartache and will make her son into a great nation. "You are to name him Ishmael (which means 'God hears'), for the LORD has heard your cry of distress," the angel says, encouraging her to return to her master (Gen. 16:11).

"You are the God who sees me," Hagar cries out in response (v. 13). The descriptive word for God Hagar uses here in the Hebrew is *El Roi*, meaning the God Who Sees.[1]

Is it an accident that the only time we see El Roi—the God Who Sees—used as a name for God in the entire Bible is here, in the middle of this slave woman's disaster? Infertility, jealousy, abuse, rage, unbelief, confusion, alienation, despair. At the bottom of this cesspool of awful circumstances beyond her control, Hagar is reassured that God *sees* her.

And isn't that what we all want? To know God sees us and doesn't look away from our pain or turn his back when our life is coming apart at the seams? To know he notices the injustice and the agony? To know he's listening when we cry out in misery, in lament?

In a few short lines we see God's reassurance that he *sees* and he *hears*. It's a display of profound presence for the moment, and a promise pregnant with hope for the future.

This same God—El Roi—is the one who meets us in our grief too. Hagar's problems aren't magically diffused through this encounter. In fact, she's sent straight back into them. But she goes fueled with hope—a reimagined vision for the future.

Can you perceive it, friends—this hope? Do you dare believe God is present in your pain, holding something hopeful for your future too?

Christian lament always comes laced with the hope that although things are not as they should be, they *will* be.

> We collapse in the dust,
> > lying face down in the dirt.
> Rise up! Help us!
> > Ransom us because of your unfailing love.
> > > (Ps. 44:25–26)

Even there in the dust, God is present. He *sees*. He *hears*. And he will not leave us in the wilderness to die.

> But forget all that—
> > it is nothing compared to what I am going to do.
> For I am about to do something new.
> > See, I have already begun! Do you not see it?
> I will make a pathway through the wilderness.
> > I will create rivers in the dry wasteland. (Isa. 43:18–19)

The Incarnation Is God's Answer to Suffering

"Who can take away suffering without entering it?" Henri Nouwen asks.[2]

In the Gospel of John we learn that there was a time when all was dark. But before that: Christ Jesus. Everything that now exists does so by his word. Where we see light, it's because of him. He is light and life itself, and in him there is no darkness.[3]

Eugene Peterson says that Jesus "became flesh and blood, and moved into the neighborhood."[4] This wasn't just an intervention to fix something broken and be on his way to solve the next cosmic problem. This was incarnation—full immersion into our earthly reality. Jesus *moved in*. He was reborn into human form so he could make our home his—humanity and divinity, born right into the middle of our suffering.

It was, and is, a miracle.

God's answer to our human condition was to become a part of it.[5]

We didn't recognize him though. And to prove we didn't recognize him, we kept right on confusing the source of our darkness with the source of our light. (We're still doing it today—blaming our good God for works of evil.) We couldn't, and can't, see clearly through our own lofty opinions about what a Messiah should look like.

But rather than coming with the law to correct us, Jesus *showed* us what Love looks like instead.[6]

The incarnation demonstrates two important things about how God relates to us in our suffering: *He is present with us in it* and *he is moved with compassion to alleviate it.*

Empathy means to stand with someone in their pain, to bear witness, to hold space, to adopt their frame of reference, or—to use the well-known cliché—to put yourself in their shoes. It's the ministry of presence, embodiment, identification, solidarity. It's the willingness to weep with the brokenhearted.

When Jesus met Mary and Martha after the death of their brother, Lazarus, their agony moved him to tears. John 11:35 lays it out with poignant simplicity:

"Jesus wept."

This word for "wept," *dakruó*, is used only once in the entire Bible to describe the quiet tears that fell that day.[7]

Imagine that—tears shed, a demonstration of empathy, emotion, and pain—juxtaposed next to *Jesus*, whose name means *Yahweh is salvation*.[8] Let this sink deep: The God of our salvation also sheds tears over our pain. He is power and presence, the lion and the lamb.[9] His ability to encompass it all is staggering.

When Mary and others were weeping, a different word is used, *klaió*, which means audible grief, weeping aloud, and weeping fueled by mourning.[10] Though Jesus didn't *mourn* the death of Lazarus (because he knew resurrection was coming), he was *moved to tears* by the pain of his friends.

Jesus enters our lament and weeps for our pain. He bears witness to our suffering. He sees us crumpled at his feet, hears our wailing, and draws near.[11]

When you started to bleed, when you repeated those words "no heartbeat" to your husband, when you were wheeled into the operating theater, when you looked your three-year-old in the eye and told him the baby was dead, when you cried yourself to sleep, Jesus was there. He wept.

The LORD is close to the brokenhearted. (Ps. 34:18)

God's presence brings comfort, but, miraculously, this "withness" in our suffering also *moves* him to act.

Out of the Darkness

"What if this darkness is not the darkness of the tomb, but the darkness of the womb?"[12]

When Valerie Kaur offered this poetic metaphor at an interfaith gathering, my heart leapt at the possibility. I couldn't help but see Jesus—whose creative power brings life out of death—between the lines of her prayer.

Like you, I have experienced a great darkness. My miscarriages exposed me to a depth of sorrow that, at times, felt like a tomb. Dark, closed, suffocating—holding within its walls an invitation to hopelessness.

But what if instead of looking at our brokenness as a tomb we see it as a womb—a place of formation and preparation for new life—even there in the suffering? What if suffering creates a cavern within us that makes room for God to form something new? What if it can enlarge our soul to make space for something bigger? What if death must precede a resurrection?

I realize this metaphor might be painful for you and me, but it's here among this darkness that the possibility for something new rests. Our bodies may have turned a womb into a tomb, but God turns death inside out. He makes our tomb into a womb—a place of resurrection, formation, and preparation for new life.

God did not lead you into this present suffering, but he *has* promised he'll stay with you there. He's promised to mend every broken thing. This is the hope of resurrection.

The incarnation shows us his presence, but it also answers our cry for deliverance.

Jesus: Man of Suffering, Man of Compassion

Throughout the Gospels, we see how Jesus was "moved with compassion" by the lament of those laboring under pain. *Compassion* comes from a Latin word meaning "co-suffering," or "to suffer with," and carries with it a sense of *movement to alleviate*.[13]

We see this compassion—this "suffering with"—moving Jesus to miraculous action all through his public ministry.

Jesus suffered with us (was "moved with compassion") when we were hungry, and so he fed us.[14] He suffered with us when we were blind, and so he made us see.[15] He suffered with us when we didn't know where to turn for help, and so became our help.[16] He suffered with us when we were oppressed by evil spirits, and so delivered us.[17] Through storytelling he taught us about "suffering with" during the long wait to welcome back those who had abandoned us.[18] He taught us to suffer with those facing the consequences of sin and to use our power to extend mercy and forgiveness, even though they hadn't earned it.[19]

The Greek word for *compassion* used in these passages, *splagchnizomai*, is sometimes also translated as "to show pity" or "to extend mercy."[20] While we may think of *pity* as having negative connotations (i.e., "self-pity" or "pity party"), we see in the Gospels that whenever Jesus is described as having compassion or pity, it always *moved* him to alleviate suffering. It was a form of love in action—a foreshadowing, even, of what he was to do on the cross.

Christian compassion is more than a feeling; it's the beginning of a movement to right what's been wrong. The root of the word also means "from the bowel," which denotes the source as coming from deep within the human heart. In all of these examples Jesus was moved deeply to enter into our suffering and birth a miracle there.

His Promise in Our Suffering

When we read these stories of Jesus today, do we forget that this man among our pages is God himself—this God who suffers with us and is *moved* to alleviate our suffering? Jesus was—and is—the full representation of the Father.[21] He's the clearest picture we have of God, but sometimes we still forget.

Sometimes we see him and think he's the "nice guy" who's covering for a God we can't understand. We claim "God's ways are higher than our ways"[22] and accuse him of causing or allowing us to suffer, despite the incarnation that shows us the exact opposite is true: God himself was born into our mess so he could turn it upside down.

He didn't make the mess. He didn't "allow" the mess. He overturned it and redeemed it.

Suffering can be the exact thing that brings you into deeper communion with Christ *because that's how redemption works*: It uses the foolish to confound the wise. It turns ashes into beauty. It makes dead things come alive. It lights up the dark with his light. It brings about good from what was started by evil.

This is our promise for suffering: In our deepest anguish, he is there, present. And at the bottom of our sorrow, he is working to make all things new. We may not see the resolution of this promise in the ways or time frame we'd like, but that doesn't negate his redemption plan: resurrection, new life, no more tears, the hope of heaven.

Don't ever think you've been abandoned in your pain. Don't ever think he will allow it to be wasted. Don't ever think your tomb can't be reworked and transformed to birth life. Don't ever think your lament is in vain. Don't ever think hope is dead.

He is present, weeping with you. He is active, shaping history toward ultimate redemption. Resurrection doesn't render death as inconsequential; it means that death doesn't have the final word.

Our Astonishing Hope

Friend, the Bible is full of astonishing hope for you and me as we suffer under the burden of our heartbreak and loss.

Paul tells us that nothing, not even our suffering, can separate us from God's love.[23] We are loved, completely. And held, strongly.

Jesus tells us we can have peace in our suffering.[24] He will overcome every hint of sorrow and death. His promises aren't empty.

James tells us suffering is an opportunity for growth and that help is available to us as we need it.[25] Our infinitely creative God will never stop creating life from dust—no suffering is wasted. This, too, can become our blessing and even a pathway to joy.

Peter tells us we'll be restored after our suffering[26] and Paul tells us that what's ahead defies our wildest imagination.[27] Suffering is not the end of our story.

God didn't take your baby, and he didn't specifically "allow" your baby to die either. Death entered the world through the free will of humankind. Life entered, again, through Jesus Christ.

Be assured, friend, that even your most awful sorrow is not beyond his redemptive reach. He can, does, and will draw near to you in your suffering; he can, does, and will bring meaning to it. He'll release his grace to the exact measure you need and will use every means possible to redeem your broken heart.[28] This is his promise.

> When you go through deep waters,
>   I will be with you.
> When you go through rivers of difficulty,
>   you will not drown.
> When you walk through the fire of oppression,
>   you will not be burned up;
>   the flames will not consume you. (Isa. 43:2)

Suffering may weaken you, but let it also awaken you as you open your heart to hope, possibility, and presence. May you find yourself in his love and let your belovedness inform your response to suffering.

During the next section we'll spend several chapters looking at the nature of grief, how to cope with and grow through your grief, and how to relate to others during your grieving journey.

As we do so, take this assurance with you: God is present in our suffering, and grief doesn't have to become our undoing. You are not alone, and your story isn't over.

Part II
Invitation

Journal Prompt: Read through the Gospel of John chapter 1 slowly, several times, prayerfully letting the story and ideas sink into your mind and spirit. As you read it three or four times, you may begin to notice a verse or two "pop out" at you. Focus in on those few lines. Chew on them, savor them. What is God trying to say to you about his presence in your brokenness? Have you felt like God has seen and heard you in your distress? Write out why or why not. Ask God to help you imagine where he was when you first learned of your miscarriage and write it down. (Imagination is a gift from God—allow him to use it for his purposes!) Ask God to show you where he is now. Write out what you see, feel, sense, or imagine.

Part III

Adrift

NAVIGATING THE WAVES
OF GRIEF

five

Diary of a Broken Heart

"$\mathcal{H}$er absence is like the sky, spread over everything," wrote C. S. Lewis after the death of his wife.[1]

I felt that absence too. It hung over everything, especially after my initiation into grief when we lost Scarlett. The ache persisted, shape-shifting its form but constantly present.

My grief would not, could not be contained within anything resembling tidy. Up and down and round and round—it was wild, untamable, confusing.

I wonder if you can see yourself in any of these journal entries?

Day 4: Holy Ground

We are talking of the future, my love and I, and recounting our short days with her and celebrating her and sharing her brief life with those we love and those we've never met. It all feels so bright—so hopeful—and I wonder if I should feel this measure of joy so soon.

Can I grieve and give thanks in one breath? Can I both cry and laugh? Feel pain unspeakably and joy unashamedly? Because I am.

There are moments of quiet when I remember the unexpected emptiness of my belly and I reach and rub and whisper I miss you while the tears come flooding again. And then I turn and see images of newborn treasures in the arms of dear friends and I feel yes. Yes, it is good—show me more, let me see.

I give thanks in my sadness and it feels right.

This ground is holy and I dare not put my shoes on for fear of marring it. I want to stay here forever and I want to run and never look back. (Can I do both?)

Day 6: The Pull

Today I'm feeling the pull between wanting to slip into denial—pretending that nothing ever happened and busying myself to help me forget—and wanting to listen to sad songs and watch sad movies and read sad stories and just cry and cry and cry and be sad, sad, sad. (Can feeling sad feel good?)

I'm tired of bleeding, cramping, hurting. Since my body no longer belongs to her, I want to take it back. Even my own flesh is caught in the murkiness of this grief. The pull is confusing.

My world feels quiet today. It's harder to hear comfort. I can't sleep at night. Or maybe I don't want to? I'm not sure. The darkness brings sadness but also covers and comforts me. The hush soothes my soul.

To miss someone so badly whom we knew so briefly—the cruelty of it all feels heavy tonight.

Come, Jesus. I know you're here. But come nearer.

Day 9: Who Cares?

I've felt a lot of anger these past few days. Anger and a vague, flat sadness intermixed.

It's not the anger I assumed would come with this sort of grieving: anger at God or at myself or at anyone in particular. It's just anger.

I'm angry because friends haven't responded the way I thought they would or should. I'm angry that life goes on and people move on, even when I'm hurting and drowning. I'm angry hearing about politicians and celebrities and this and that related to work or ministry or culture and I just think Who cares?! Why does any of it matter when my child is dead?! And what on earth is Twitter for, anyway?! *It makes me angry—all of it.*

But under my anger is pain. The sadness hurts. I'm dreading so many things right now: my first period, the lab results, her due date, Mother's Day, Tuesday. That thin place I spoke of last week—it's wearing off. Was there a "high" that came with the sudden influx of emotions? It's harder for me to feel God now. It's harder for me to hear.

Day 11: More Than Her

I don't feel as angry today. But I know it comes in waves.

Yesterday I had so many moments of calm followed closely by rage. I'd look at my boys and want to cover them with kisses—do they know how much I love them? I need them to know. *But then would come intense moments of anger. Stop fighting. Stop whining. Stop spilling. Stop yelling. Stop needing me. Please. Just. STOP.*

I desperately want them to need me and want me and desire to be close to me. And yet I also want them far away so I can think and pray and hear the stillness. I want my house clean and my world quiet. But I never want to let them go.

I've been "angry at the world," I tell Ryan. Angry at anything even remotely "worthy" of getting angry about. It's like my subconscious is just waiting for something to pounce on—something to blame for making life so hard.

I can't blame God. I just can't. He's too good to me. I don't want to blame myself. I'm already hurting too much. So I just want to blame everyone and everything else for the pain.

Then my logic kicks in and I realize I'm grieving and my emotions—though real—can't be trusted. There's no one to be angry at. No one to shoulder the blame. I'm just angry, and it's okay. It will pass. Or maybe I'll pass through it. Even there, he will be with me.

But today—this moment—I don't feel angry. I feel calm. I feel sad. I feel hopeful. The sun will shine again. (It's already trying.)

My world hasn't changed—purpose is still there—but I've changed and that's a good thing. I'm still changing.

Jesus, I need you to know: I love you even more than I loved her.

Day 14: Stormy

It's stormy here today. I adjust my sails and attempt to work within the waves. But it's hard. It's really hard.

Jesus, it's so damn hard.

Day 15: Oceans

I feel so vague, so remiss, so lost.

Where do I live again? What's the teacher's name at Levi's preschool? Did I push start on the fully loaded dishwasher?

I can't explain why the furniture needs rearranging and the garage needs cleaning.

I can't explain why I need to browse the baby aisles, touching onesies and searching for God-knows-what.

I can't explain why simple household tasks make me cry or why I'm so tired, so fragile, so quiet.

I can't explain how out of sorts I feel in my own body.

I'm still in the ocean. Waves and waves and riptides and calm and more waves. I feel like I'm drowning but I'm not. Salt water is good for wounds, you know. But I don't feel healed yet; it all just stings.

Day 18: Go Deep

Today I wondered about that milestone day sometime in the future when I don't cry about losing her. When will it be? Is it close? Distant?

I don't want to rush this time. As much as I want to fast-forward or rewind or somehow find an easier place, I sense deep calling to deep. Is this some sort of awakening?

Oh, baby girl, we miss you. We love you.

Day 40: Mother's Day

I've felt thin today—fragile, vulnerable, a little bit weepy. I've been hurt by small things and let down by things said and unsaid.

I'm struggling with walking in rejection—feeling forgotten and hurt. But I know it's the state of my own heart, not the fault of others. This, too, is grief.

There's an ache in my soul, a longing for more. I keep giving names to it, but really . . . it's heaven. I'm aching and longing for heaven. This isn't my home.

Mother's Day, I see you. Do you see me too?

Grief Cannot Be Conquered—It Must Be Lived

Sometimes grief feels like rain. You can't stop it, but you learn to manage in the midst of it. When the storm clouds break overhead, it's not enough for someone to acknowledge you're wet. That's a good start, but what you actually need is an umbrella. Empathy is when someone steps into the rain with you and hands you an umbrella; it's a willingness to make your pain their own and share the load. Empathy says, "I see you and I'm with you in this," and then demonstrates what that looks like in actual practice. My friend Greg calls this "sideways living."[2]

After losing Scarlett, Levi taught me the power of sideways living best.

Sometimes "Yeah" Is Exactly Right

It was an impossibly spectacular day—the kind you'd be crazy not to take your kids to the park for—and it was there I saw her.

She had cut my hair nearly a year before at the drop-in salon I ducked into at the mall (because I'm fancy like that). I remembered liking her and having easy conversation about her family in Sri Lanka and her husband working his way through university here in Australia.

Now, at the neighborhood park, we watched our boys bonding over the pirate ship play structure, delighting in the way children become such fast friends.

"Do you have other kids?" I asked, initiating small talk.

"Just my son," she paused, patting her belly, "and a baby on the way."

I smiled.

"Due October 12," she added.

My eyes welled with tears under my sunglasses. She had just named Scarlett's due date. Even though my heart was breaking all over again, I kept smiling and told her, "Congratulations, that's wonderful," because it *was*.

Boom. Downpour. I didn't see it coming on that gorgeous, sunny day.

While driving home from the park I cried in silence behind my dark glasses, hoping the boys couldn't see my wet cheeks from the backseat. (I didn't want to hide my grief from them, but I didn't want to burden them either.)

"Why are you sad, Mommy?" three-year-old Levi asked. (I'm still not sure how he knew.) "Because you want the baby to come home?"

"Yes," I gasped. "Yes." I paused to catch my breath. "I just want the baby to come home. I miss her."

"Yeah," he said tenderly before going quiet again.

Sometimes the best thing for a grieving heart is for someone to say *yeah* and validate how hard it all is. We don't need to be fixed; we just need to be accepted in our brokenness. My three-year-old taught me that—he handed me an umbrella while I drove home in the rain on that sunny day.

Sideways living is all about embodying Jesus to the people around us. It means entering into their world—their hardships, their challenges, their victories, their grief, their joy, all of it—and letting them enter into ours.

I still find it hard to understand how you can feel so lonely while also feeling the comforting presence of Jesus, but my grief experience showed me it's possible. Even now as I write, I try to imagine myself entering into your own wild up-and-down, round-and-round grief experience, handing you an umbrella and saying "I'm with you, sister." I hope you have people in your life saying something similar. But if you don't, let me say it for them: Miscarriage is painful and your grief is warranted. You loved hard, so you'll grieve hard too. And that's okay. Consider this your permission to feel what you feel without trying to run away.

The Nature of Grief Is Not Linear

A hundred years ago I learned about the stages of grief in an entry-level psychology class. I vaguely remember the stages: shock and denial, anger and blame, bargaining, depression, and acceptance. The problem with calling these "stages"—I was later to learn—is that it implies a linear process to work through in order to come out the other side "all better." No grief expert would ever tell you this is how it works, but I wonder how many of us "regular" people have misunderstood these stages.

Having no experiential framework to understand these concepts, I imagined grief to be a straightforward line of steps to be worked through—a trajectory to take one back to his or her "normal" self. The quicker one came to acceptance, the sooner the pain would be "dealt with" and life could go on. This explanation resonated with my problem-solving, fix-it sensibilities, and I went years as an adult without these ideas being challenged.

It made no sense, then, that the day following my D&C with Scarlett I was on the beach eating ice cream with my family, hearts full as we reflected on the many blessings in our lives despite our loss. We felt so *normal*, happy even. Could it be that we had already reached the acceptance stage? Or did this mean we were in denial of what just happened? I remember trying to psychoanalyze my own grief so I could figure out where I was on the trajectory and when I might be finished. (*Whomp whomp.*)

The most dangerous myth about grief is that it's linear and ordered and predictable—that it can be confined and conquered. The problem with this line of thinking is that when you stray from the supposed order of operations, you're immediately tempted to assume you're not "doing it right." (Aaaand . . . let the berating and self-loathing commence. Ugh.)

Ryan and I experienced a feeling of tangible grace for the first several days after each of our miscarriages. We're convinced it had to do with the many people holding our hearts in prayer before the

Lord. (Note: Homemade chocolate chip cookies also help. Amen.) The presence of Jesus was breathtaking during those precious, excruciating days. His nearness in our brokenness was as real as the emptiness of my womb.

Perhaps that's why it shocked me so much that soon after those first tender days I would find myself struggling with despair one day, waking up with rage the next, and feeling mostly indifferent the day after that. I mean, couldn't Jesus fix this? Why didn't I always feel that sweet, steadying presence? Why did I feel so knocked around?

No doubt this is why the metaphor "waves of grief" is such common language among the grief community. You never really know how or when grief is going to hit you with the force of a tsunami or lap against your ankles quietly. It's disorienting and engulfing and surprising. Even the apostle Peter described "sorrow upon sorrow" (Phil. 2:27 ESV), hinting at the wave imagery when describing his own heartache.

Grief as a Story

Because grief is not linear, you can't work your way through the stages, crossing them off a list as you go. In my experience, it feels more circular, like going around and around the same mountain. *Didn't I already deal with my anger? Didn't I already go through depression? I've been here before, right?* But since grief is not linear, we don't have to be panicked by the seeming repetition. A better question to ask, then, would be *Am I spiraling up or down as I go round this mountain again?*

Psychotherapist Patrick O'Malley says the assumption that grief is linear can hinder the healing process and suggests thinking of your loss as a story instead.

> When loss is a story, there is no right or wrong way to grieve. There is no pressure to move on. There is no shame in intensity or duration.

Sadness, regret, confusion, yearning and all the experiences of grief become part of the narrative of love for the one who died.[3]

After experiencing multiple miscarriages, I found this way of explaining grief resonates with me so much and helps me understand why each of my miscarriages caused such different grief responses. I hope it helps *you* understand your grief, too, because when you know you're normal, it's much easier to give yourself grace for the process.

As I've met and corresponded with thousands of parents who've experienced miscarriage, stillbirth, infertility, abortion, and other types of loss, I've been simultaneously astonished and relieved to hear the many shapes and forms their grief has taken. Although there are *certainly* common threads, there is also not a single story that fits every bereaved parent.

six

A Thousand Shades of Grief

The most surprising thing about my grief was how surprising it was. I would be cruising along fine one day and then feel run over by a monster truck the next. I never knew what to expect.

Annalyn

While researching this book, I surveyed more than 750 bereaved moms and dads.[1] One of the open-ended questions I asked was *What surprised you most about your grief?* Two common answers emerged: how isolating the experience felt and how deep their sorrow was. After those two, the rest of the answers ranged as wide as the Nebraska plains. Here's just a sample:

How much I blamed myself

How uncontrollable my grief felt

How bonded I felt to a baby I never knew

That I didn't feel entitled to grieve

How all-encompassing it was

How relieved I was

How devastated I was

How much I felt at peace even while being incredibly sad

The amount of things that served as triggers for my grief

How embarrassed I felt

How much I wanted to cry but couldn't

How angry I was

How let down I felt by my friends

How differently my husband/wife grieved

That I felt like an utter failure

How much I longed for a substance to numb the pain

How much guilt I had

That I struggled to feel much at all

How much I hated my body

How little I grieved until the birth of my next baby, when all
my grief came pouring out

How close to God I felt

How far from God I felt

That I still cry years later

How ashamed I felt

How dismissive people were

How much it affected our sex life and intimacy

How much grief made me yearn to be a mother

The way I struggled with normal things like cooking dinner
and taking the trash out

How afraid I was to get pregnant again

How obsessed I was with getting pregnant again

How annoyed I felt by my living children

How much healing my living children gave me

How quickly I questioned things I had always believed about
God

How common it is and how many people I know who've experienced the same thing

That I had an intense need for privacy

That I had an overwhelming need for company

How tired I felt all the time

How thankful I became for the other good things in my life

How distant I felt from my husband

How close I felt to my husband

How uncomfortable others seemed to feel around me

How much I hated people who had never experienced this

How depressed I became

How quickly I wanted to move on

How awful I felt around pregnant mothers and babies

How guilty I felt to laugh

How much I wanted to hurt myself

How alone I felt when going to church

How much I grew in my faith

As you can see, these responses are all over the place. My point
here is there's no neat and tidy grief box we can pack our experiences into. Having lost three babies to miscarriage myself, I can
personally attest to the fact that there's no uniformity to grief, even
within the heart of a single person, much less spread throughout
the human experience.

When we lost Scarlett we were blindsided. It was the most sad,
tragic, unexpected event of our lives. That loss was characterized
most by sorrow.

When we lost Oliver we were blindsided again. We genuinely
thought our first miscarriage was a one-off and were truly shocked
to be thrust into the pain all over again. Although there was sadness surrounding our loss, we felt more anger than anything else.
We felt robbed and violated by what seemed like such injustice.

We were angry it had happened at all, angry it had happened in Italy while I was on the "trip of a lifetime," angry people around us didn't show up the way we thought they would (or should), angry we had to go through the grieving process again, angry we had no understanding—no physical explanation of why this was happening. The whole thing felt like a mounting avalanche of anger.

But losing Ruby, our third miscarriage, was different yet again.

When Grief Feels like . . . Nothing

My first miscarriage was in Australia in far northeast Queensland, and my second was split between Italy and Oregon (where we lived during our ministry sabbatical). The third happened when we were living in a 95-square-foot caravan[2] in our friends' driveway in Perth, on the *other* side of Australia.

So as you can see, my family was rootless at the time—in a seismic transition from one ministry and state to another—but tragedy doesn't wait until a good time. It interrupts without discretion.

While visiting friends on our long drive west, we took communion together and ended our time in prayer. During prayer I sensed God's whisper that he would give us another baby girl. We would name her Ruby to remind us of God's promise from Isaiah 54 to rebuild Jerusalem with precious jewels. I kept this to myself, and again we entered the emotionally fraught territory of trying to conceive.

When the pink lines appeared soon after, I was terrified and anxious. I was excited to be pregnant—believing, again, that our baby was a gift from God—but two miscarriages in a row had left me feeling like a statistical misfit. Deep in my bones I felt like my body wasn't responding as it should.

Though I wanted to, I struggled to free-fall into love or dream of a future with this baby. Instead, I put my energy into finding a doctor willing to order early pregnancy screenings.

I booked a dating scan and had my hormone levels checked. The scan measured me as five weeks along; I knew I should have measured seven. My pregnancy hormone levels were far below what they should have been. They sent me home to wait, so, like the obedient patient I am, I went to the emergency department at the women's hospital and pleaded to see someone who would take my suspicions seriously. Perhaps there was no blood to prove it, but I was losing the child and I knew it.

They admitted me, and it was true: another little body without a heartbeat. Before I ever started to bleed, I booked another D&C. I couldn't bear to wait in limbo, possibly for weeks, for my uterus to catch up to what the rest of me knew. I needed my dead baby out.

I felt numb, like an empty shell of a woman whose body had fallen apart without giving notice.

The Best of the Worst

The D&C went smoothly and easily—I was assigned a good surgeon who was as skilled at bedside manner as she was at scraping me clean. I can't even remember her name, but when she kneeled down to eye level by my chair to go through the presurgery protocol, I immediately loved her and felt safe with her. She was gentle and compassionate and made me feel human, not simply another woman in a robe lined up for a common medical procedure.

It seems strange to say, but my third miscarriage was the best of the three. I realize *best* is a ridiculous term to use within these circumstances, but something about having "known" things were wrong from the start helped ease the trauma. That, coupled with a straightforward hospital experience, helped me come to terms with the fact that I had become an anomaly—I was now classified with "recurrent miscarriages" and plopped by the medical profession squarely into the infertility camp.

There *was* something wrong with me. I had no idea how to process that.

Of all my miscarriages, this one was the most expected, most swift, and most well cared for. I didn't know how to feel the sorrow and anger in the same way I had before. Mostly I just felt defeated. Why bother trying to grow our family, regardless of what we believed God had said?

Genetic testing confirmed our baby was, indeed, a girl, and we smiled at the news, having already named her Ruby Hannah. (The boys chose Hannah, which we liked; it seemed fitting to name her after a woman of heartache and hope.[3])

Tests also confirmed there was nothing wrong with her. For the third time we had no answers.

Small and Hushed

While losing Scarlett and Oliver left me with a compulsion to write volumes, by the time I lost Ruby my well was dry.

What does a mother say after the third death of a baby? There were no words left. I had already begun work on this book, but in my despondency I put it all away, leaving the manuscript to gather dust on the shelf along with my dreams.

If there were words in my heart, they must have been buried deep, because nothing surfaced for months. In fact, six months passed before I could pick up a pen, and even then it was reluctantly, knowing my soul needed room to breathe and that my soul-breathing often took the shape of writing. I needed to write in order to grieve.

Writing wasn't the only thing that went quiet over that time. God seemed quiet too. I didn't know how to hear him. I didn't know how to speak. I grappled with the "shoulds" of prayer but felt no desire to push past the silence and try to connect in that way.

I barely prayed during those months of dull grief, at least not in the "Dear Jesus" way. When I did it felt like dragging a wheelbarrow through mud—heavy, slow, difficult. I had to learn to make peace with the silence and believe God was still present even when I didn't know how to feel him. (I had not yet learned how to pray the liturgy but I imagine this spiritual practice would have been life-giving to me during this period.[4])

God continued to show me goodness, so I knew he was there, but everything was shadowy. Those long, muted months taught me that honest prayer can sometimes be formed with no words at all as we lean in and embrace the comforting knowledge that the Holy Spirit intercedes for us.[5]

I was tired—overwhelmingly so. My grief was buried under fatigue, and I realized that weariness is a form of sorrow disguised. I needed to give permission for my quietness to *be* without trying to manipulate it into something productive or "helpful" to the grieving process. Being quiet and tired made me feel numb, and feeling numb made me feel tired. I wondered if I was depressed.

During that time I visited a professional counselor. Surely there was more buried under the surface, I thought to myself. Three miscarriages in three years is a lot of heartache. But as I shared pieces of my story with the counselor week after week, I felt removed—like the story included me but didn't move me. I just didn't feel the grief like I had before. I kept hoping to, as if feeling *something* would make me feel *better.*

After four or five sessions the psychologist said she didn't need to see me anymore unless I wanted to. She thought I was coping and healing "just fine." I left in agreement with her—I was "fine"— but I still wondered if there was more to it. I wanted to feel deep sadness or hot anger—anything that would stir my soul. I wanted to give better expression to the void in my mother's heart. Didn't my daughter deserve that?

In retrospect, I'm pretty sure I had mild depression. I'm not sure why the psychologist couldn't see it, but I stumbled along, quiet in my grief and caring for my soul the best I could. I continued to give God the "faintest yes" while he stayed with me in my grief.

This was the only way I could grieve the loss of Ruby: small and hushed. I could only grieve the way I could grieve. And so can you. We can't force an expression of grief; we can only live the one that's authentic.

So tell me: What is it *your* heart longs to give expression to? Is it loud and large? Small and silent? How can you own your grief in this season and let it run its natural course in the safe presence of Jesus? There is no "right" way forward, but there *is* a way forward.

Let Grief Transform You

I've come to learn that grief must be swallowed—*not* to make it disappear but to let it absorb into us, become a part of us, change us, and nurture us from the inside out. It will change the way you relate to others, the way you watch the news, read your Bible, pray. It will change your expectations of yourself, your marriage, your work, your parenting, the way you see God, even the metaphors you use for your life. In all of these things, turn toward Jesus and let grief shape you like him. This, too, is spiritual formation.

The Bible teaches us that anything (your grief included!) can be redeemed for our good if we're willing to cooperate. "We know that in everything God works for good *with those* who love him, who are called according to his purpose" (Rom. 8:28 RSV, emphasis mine). The original Greek word we translate into *work* here (*sunergeó*), actually means "coworking; being a partner with; or working together," meaning God isn't just going to rescue us from the mess and make something good out of it, he's going to *partner with us* to see good come about.[6] We aren't his project to fix; we're *cocreators* of something good. We're in this together. What hope we have!

No one can prescribe the way forward for you, but there *is* a way forward—ask Jesus to lead you and do what brings peace to your soul. You can't expect to simply "get over" the loss of your child, but you will get through the days of heavy grief—not by skirting around them but by stepping straight in and embracing the process with Jesus. Grant yourself permission to go at your own pace. Allow yourself the freedom to feel what you feel without trying to quantify or qualify your pain. Your humanity isn't a burden to God; it's a gift that will keep you tethered to him. Stay close. Dive deep. Create something good together.

Grieving Well

As I close this section, I want to pose a few questions and offer some suggestions, but you've got to know this whole thing must be immersed in grace. There is no "right" way to grieve, but I believe you can find a way to grieve *well*. Remember: Grief is a process, not a project.

Let's start here: What might it look like for you to grieve well? How might you make peace with your grief while it works its way through your mind and heart? Are you willing to deep dive into the presence of Jesus in the midst of those pounding waves, knowing that sometimes you can't hear him under there? In what ways do you need to give yourself grace as you heal?

There are healthy and unhealthy ways to grieve—healthy, constructive coping mechanisms and unhealthy, destructive ones. Giving yourself permission to feel sad and depressed is not the same thing as refusing to get out of bed for weeks on end. Confessing your feelings of anger or rage is different than unleashing them on loved ones. Running to relieve tension is different than running away from the people who care about you most. Eating comfort foods that nurture you from the inside is different than medicating your pain with a freezer full of ice cream. Having a glass of wine and a heart-to-heart with your girlfriend is different than hiding a bottle of gin in the closet.

How will you cope when the grief feels consuming? What are the things that might bring life to your soul?

You might find, like me, that writing helps you to process your grief, or that listening to (or playing) music feeds your soul. You might need to join a support group or Bible study. You might need to make a memory box, or leave the baby things out until you're ready to say goodbye, or pack them up straightaway. You may need to speak to a professional counselor or take antidepressants so you can process your grief with a clearer mind. You may need to commit to a practice of scripture meditation or regular journaling or centering prayer. Do you need to arm yourself with scientific and medical knowledge? Do you need to dig into the Bible to solidify your theology of heaven? Do you need to join an online support forum and walk alongside other grieving mothers?

Remember, grieving "well" is not the same thing as grieving "right." To grieve well means to find yourself within Jesus even when you're taking these intentional steps of self-care.

Live your grief. If you are willing to embrace your loss and heartache and pain, you'll be able to own your grief without letting your grief own you. God's grace doesn't heal you *from* grief; it heals you *as you grieve* and then right through to the other side.

You Are Not Alone

Be honest about your pain and your grief—with yourself, your loved ones, and God. Walking through grief together with trusted loved ones is a disarmingly powerful fellowship—a joy entangled in the pain. I pray you'll discover the fullness of that experience. We were never meant to grieve alone.

Even Jesus himself needed his closest friends while experiencing profound sorrow.

They went to the olive grove called Gethsemane, and Jesus said, "Sit here while I go and pray." He took Peter, James, and John with him, and he became deeply troubled and distressed. He told them, "My soul is crushed with grief to the point of death. Stay here and keep watch with me." (Mark 14:32–34)

There are a thousand shades of grief, but Jesus understands every single one. He will meet you in the deep and will stay there with you as long as it takes. Forever, actually. You will never be alone.

> My flesh and my heart may fail,
>> but God is the strength of my heart and my portion
>>> forever. (Ps. 73:26 ESV)

Part III
Invitation

Journal Prompt: Write a letter to yourself, granting yourself permission to let go of any unrealistic expectations you have about grief, and to feel and grieve in the presence of Jesus. If you're able, identify things that might stifle your grieving process and bring them before the Lord. This is also a good time to consider what will help you grieve well. Do you need to share your story with a friend, with a support group, or more widely (such as a personal blog or social media post)? Do you need to speak with your health-care provider about seeing a counselor or to assess the need for other health measures (such as medication)? Do you need to reach out to your husband and be more honest about how your miscarriage is affecting you? Even if you're still looking for the answers to these questions, write yourself permission to explore your grief and find your way within it.

Part IV

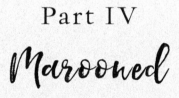

Marooned

THE ISOLATION
OF BEREAVEMENT

seven

The Eighteen-Inch Journey

I stared at myself in the mirror, repulsed by the girl I saw. I wasn't pregnant or unpregnant. Our baby was gone, but my body didn't get the memo. My breasts were leaking milk, I felt covered in blood, my waist had expanded two pants sizes, and yet I was empty. No baby. I've never felt like such a failure in my whole life. This one thing that's meant to distinguish us as women, or so I thought, was the one thing I couldn't manage: I simply couldn't stay pregnant. I felt so ashamed and embarrassed and ugly. It took all my reserves just to show my face to the world—go to work, attend church—much less get naked with my husband. I just wanted to hide all of my mess. I felt unlovely *and* unlovable.

Megan

Every time someone found out I had a miscarriage, the first question they asked was, "How far along were you?" And every single time I felt ashamed to say "seven weeks," as if the short length of my pregnancy meant it mattered less and shouldn't have affected me so much.

Dana

Shame corrodes us. It corrodes our confidence, our sense of worth, our ability to give and receive love, our understanding of justice, our freedom, our courage. It corrodes our ability to see clearly. It's an acid to our souls and will undercut our relationships if we leave it unattended.

Have you ever felt ashamed about your miscarriage? Of your body? Of your weakness? Of your tenuous faith? Of your response to your grief? Of yourself?

I still sometimes feel silly. Like somehow my pain—or my reaction to it—is ridiculous. This, too, is shame.

Shame Sneaks in When You're Not Looking

When I was a child, I was often called *dramatic*. And I was. I loved singing and acting and dancing and dreamed of being a Broadway star. (My backup plan was to become the next Amy Grant if Broadway didn't work out.) But somewhere in the coming-of-age process I learned that being called *dramatic* was not a compliment but an insult. It wasn't a bolster to my creativity or an encouragement to explore expression; it was a prescription to tame my "too muchness," an antidote to my big feelings, a *shush* to being me. As an adult I can now see how the childhood version of me misinterpreted and assimilated these faulty notions into my subconscious. But still, they lodged: I was *dramatic* and that made me foolish.

During a sixth-grade sleepover with friends, we played "crack the whip" in the front yard, holding hands and running as fast as we possibly could until the circle broke and one of us went flying. I was that one. I screamed in pain and cried as my friends gathered around me with mixed reactions to the accident. Mostly they said things like, "Are you okay? You'll be fine," and kept right on playing. I felt stupid for reacting to pain the way I did and tried to act like it was no big deal. According to my friends it was an unfortunate little blip. Clearly I was overreacting.

It wasn't until hours later, when they were all giggling over movies, that my friend's mother noticed me on the couch burning up with a fever. She called my dad and, soon after, an emergency room visit confirmed a fracture in my arm. See? My pain was real. But that didn't erase the fact that I felt silly for how it moved me.

I've had decades to work through a lot of the damage done to my young soul by that one little word, *dramatic*, but here's the honest truth: I'm thirty-nine years old and I still worry about being too dramatic. I still sometimes worry that others might think I'm silly. (Admitting that feels so vulnerable.)

After my first miscarriage, I wasn't ashamed of my body. I suspect already having two kids loaned courage to my belief that the miscarriage happened *to* me—this was not my fault. I wasn't ashamed by what had happened, or even my part in it, but I *did* struggle to not be ashamed by how I felt. I simply couldn't harness my agony. It was wild, and I hoped that didn't make me ridiculous.

No one told me so, but I felt like my reaction was *dramatic*. I felt like my loneliness was *dramatic*. I felt like my despair was *dramatic*. I felt like my suffering was *dramatic*. I felt like my unrelenting tears were *dramatic*. The immensity of my own emotions frightened me, but they also whispered back to me: *You're being dramatic. This is all a bit much now, isn't it?*

I didn't need coaxing to "feel what you need to feel" or encouragement to "let yourself grieve." No, expressing the full weight of my pain and grief came easily to me; I'm demonstrative by nature. What I needed was to remember how to breathe down there at the bottom of my grief when I seriously wondered if the pressure of my own snot could explode my skull from the inside. I needed to know my visceral response was not silly. I needed to know that my full-body reaction to grief did not make me ridiculous.

Shame Is Reinforced over Time

Even if you can't pinpoint a certain childhood experience when you felt shamed, perhaps shame has woven its way into your subconscious through a series of events or words spoken over you during any stage of your life. In the words of psychiatrist Curt Thompson:

> While we may think of large, monolithic, humiliating public events, the reality is that most shame takes place inside your head dozens of times every day. It's silent, subtle, and characterized by the quiet self-condemning conversation that we've learned since we were kids.[1]

Maybe your miscarriage reinforced already existing feelings of failure or inadequacy or poor self-worth, or maybe it was the first time you ever really felt devastated by trauma, and what the trauma has exposed is surprising to you. In any case, I encourage you now to think deeply and ask yourself this question in the presence of Jesus: *Do I feel a sense of shame resulting from this miscarriage?*

Here are some specifics you might consider:

Have you felt shame about your response to grief ("too much" or "not enough")?

Have you felt shame about your body's (perceived) failure?

Have you felt shame about your womanhood?

Have you felt shame about what this crisis has revealed about your faith or perception of God?

Have you felt shame for not wanting the baby in the first place?

Have you felt shame that you "*mis*-carried" the baby, as if somehow it's all your fault?

Almost 30 percent of the bereaved parents I surveyed said they experienced shame after their miscarriages, and these are the ones who could easily identify it; there could be far more.

Shame tells us we are deeply flawed; not that we've *done* something wrong—that's guilt—but that we *are* wrong. Whereas guilt can be alleviated through confession, asking forgiveness, and making restitution, shame hangs around without regard to your morality. Shame says you're inherently defective, that *you* are the problem.

Stigma Surrounding Miscarriage Is a Breeding Ground for Shame

Since first experiencing miscarriage, I've often wondered why women aren't talking about it more. If it's so prevalent, why is it still such a culturally taboo topic? (And why aren't men talking about it? What about the grieving dads?) As I've turned these questions over in my mind, I keep coming back to this issue of shame. We may or may not think we've done something to cause the miscarriage (guilt), but do we know—deep in our bones—that we aren't intrinsically faulty human beings? Do we secretly think we aren't good enough? Do we fear we're deeply flawed as women?

So many things can contribute to feeling a sense of shame over miscarriages: the inconclusive nature of the loss, the lack of social validation, the societal expectation that we bear our loss in private (such as the belief that we should keep a pregnancy secret until after twelve weeks have passed), the absence of a cultural ritual to invite others to participate in mourning or commemorating a lost life, the risk of our vulnerability being judged or brushed off, the expectation that we can quickly get over it, the assumption that all women can have babies. There's a whole lot of overt *and* subtle stigma hinting that we should be ashamed.

Shame makes us turn our pain inward. Not in a constructive, soul-searching way, but in a destructive, soul-decimating way. Shame keeps a woman paralyzed in fear as she tries to convince herself and the world that "everything is okay," when really she has no idea what to do with her grief. Shame accommodates the inner critic telling her no one understands and no one cares anyway.

Shame draws us into ourselves, leads us into hiding, and keeps us separated from the very things that can bring healing: the light of Jesus and the love and acceptance of others.

The truth is when we dare to open ourselves up before others in our pain, something powerful can be birthed between us. Brené Brown calls this the "gift of vulnerability,"[2] and the writer of Hebrews calls it grace.[3] When we humble ourselves enough to let down our guard and be known for who we really are, grace is released. We are free to love and be loved.

Shame Alienates Us from Love

The first instance of shame ever recorded in human history takes place in Eden. In Genesis 2 we see that Adam and Eve were naked but not ashamed.[4] In chapter 3, after they rebelled against God, they hid from him, ashamed.[5] What caused their leap from unashamed to ashamed? It wasn't merely sin; it was the *result* of sin—separation from God. Shame alienates us from love. That's true of our relationship with God and it's true of every human relationship that exists. When we are ashamed, we are hindered in our ability to experience the fullness of the love, connection, and belonging we were created for.

When Adam and Eve's shame drove them into hiding, God's response was to call for them, draw them out, and cover them.[6] He always addresses our shame by first entering into it and then extending love. He showed us this in the garden, and again in graphic detail on the cross.

"This is why the Crucifixion and Jesus' naked body is such a big deal," says Thompson.

> Even in our artwork depicting the event, we don't strip him naked. We have a loincloth around him, and that's all well and good, but it suggests that we don't want God going that far. But he does. God himself submitted to the shame of the Cross. He has been

94

there. And he says, "I'm willing to go with you where you're not even willing to go."[7]

Shame cannot exist in the presence of love, therefore shame can't exist in the presence of God, for he *is* Love.[8] When we look into the disarming eyes of Jesus, he sees us naked and loves us anyway. Our masks are irrelevant, our coping mechanisms are rendered useless, our clichéd responses are defused of their power, and all we have left is ourselves, stripped bare of our defenses in the best possible way. Our most carefully erected fortification schemes don't stand a chance against his love. Shame is given no oxygen to breathe in the presence of love, whether human or divine, and our nakedness and vulnerability become a gift.

The Tangle of Guilt and Shame

The tentacles of guilt and shame can be difficult to untangle. With so much overlap, they can be hard to distinguish. Of my survey participants, 41 percent reported feeling guilty after their miscarriage. Listen to some of their stories:

> I felt guilty about some huge life decisions I made just before my miscarriage. Rationally I knew they weren't the cause, but I think subconsciously I was trying to assign blame somewhere and it was easy to blame myself.—Jen

> I had just started a rigorous diet and exercise program with the blessing of my doctor. Although I didn't know I was pregnant at the time, when I miscarried a few weeks later, I instantly felt guilty and believed I was responsible.—Shana

> We had two under two when I got pregnant unexpectedly, and I was already suffering from postpartum depression. I was terrified to be pregnant again and seriously considered abortion. Soon after deciding I couldn't go through with it I miscarried the baby

anyway. I felt so guilty and was sure this was God's punishment to me.—Anonymous

My husband and I were having significant problems and talking about getting a divorce when I got pregnant. The whole thing was a mess. When I miscarried I felt so relieved, but my relief came with so much guilt. Our marriage has since been reconciled, but I still struggle with the guilt surrounding the miscarriage.
—Melissa

We waited a long time before trying to have kids, mostly because I wanted to develop my career while also pursuing my PhD. When I finally agreed to try for a baby, I miscarried and felt so guilty that it was my fault. I'll always wonder if it would have happened had I not been an "older" mother. I also struggled with a lot of shame because I assumed everyone else thought it was my fault too. Like they were silently judging me for being so into my career and waiting so long.—Steph

I would sometimes make jokes about my baby in heaven. Maybe it sounds weird, but I think it's how I coped with my sadness. It helped at first, but when I was done laughing, I always felt super guilty. Like I was cheapening the experience.—Tess

We got pregnant with a honeymoon baby and we were *not* ready to be parents. Then I miscarried the baby and was reeling: Why did God let us get pregnant and then leave me heartbroken? I only knew I was pregnant for two days but suffered tremendous guilt. I didn't know how or why, but I 100 percent believed it was my fault. The guilt was suffocating, and I couldn't imagine anything good coming from a marriage that seemed so wrecked from the beginning. The whole thing was traumatic.—Naomi

As I said earlier, shame says that you *are* wrong, whereas guilt says that you've *done* something wrong. Brené Brown puts it this way: Guilt says, "I'm sorry, I made a mistake," whereas shame says, "I'm sorry, I *am* a mistake."⁹

Guilt Is Productive, False Guilt Is Destructive

Guilt can be a powerful tool to direct us toward righting our wrongs—finding forgiveness before the Lord and seeking forgiveness and reconciliation in our human relationships. In John 16:13 Jesus tells us that the Holy Spirit will guide us into truth. God works through our conscience and our spirit to convict us when we need to address wrongdoing in our lives. But there is a difference between *feeling* guilty and *being* guilty, which is why we need the Spirit's help to discern the difference.

False guilt is when we feel guilty but aren't. And guess what? Shame can drive us right into the ditch of false guilt and keep us stuck there.

It's not uncommon at all for women to feel a sense of guilt over their miscarriages. We're given laundry lists of "dos and don'ts" for pregnancy, so it seems natural to jump straight to that list after miscarriage and think, *What in the world did I do wrong? Did I miss something? Did I not follow the rules closely enough?*

Or, if we have a skewed view of God, his role in suffering, and/or his heart for us, we might think, *What did I do to deserve this? Is this some sort of divine punishment? Does God not love me enough to save my baby?*

If you've had any of these thoughts I'd like to gently take you by the shoulders, eyeball you like only a loving, protective big sister can, and tell you two things: (1) You are not responsible for your miscarriage. (2) You've got to let this idea go.

False guilt will eat away an already-broken heart if left unresolved. Whether shame led to your false guilt or not, false guilt *will* lead you to shame. And shame will wreck your relationships. It will wreck how you relate to God and to your loved ones. It will even wreck how you relate to your own soul.

Friend, the enemy of your soul would give anything to see you caught in a crippling cycle of self-loathing, self-criticism, self-doubt, and false accusation driven by a sense of guilt (false guilt!)

over circumstances that were completely out of your control. Don't give in to it. Kick the accuser[10] in the shins by asking God to show you truth.

Truth Brings Freedom

> Jesus said to the people who believed in him, "You are truly my disciples if you remain faithful to my teachings. And you will know the truth, and the truth will set you free." (John 8:31–32)

Did you catch that? The truth will set you free. But knowing the truth doesn't just come by memorizing this or that biblical principle; it comes by *obeying the teachings of Jesus*. See the order there? (Go ahead and read the scripture again.) When we remain faithful to the teachings of Jesus, we'll know truth. This knowledge—this living, breathing, experiential knowledge—will set us free. But we've got to trust him enough to obey his teachings first.

So what does he teach?

You are loved exactly as you are.[11]

He sees you as exquisite.[12]

When God looks at you, he sees Jesus.[13]

Nothing can ever separate you from his love.[14]

Every tear that's ever fallen from your broken heart will be wiped away.[15]

God is *for* you.[16]

You are worth *everything*.[17]

Are you willing to accept these teachings, sweet mama? As you do, you can, and will, be set free from the false things you're believing about yourself.

Friends of ours, the Helsers, are famous for saying that the greatest journey a person can ever make is the eighteen-inch journey from our head to our heart.[18] Do you have beliefs about yourself and about God that are disrupting your heart? Or do you "know" what God says and thinks of you in your head but haven't yet let that knowledge become living and breathing as a transformative truth buried in your heart?

As you're dealing with the carnage left behind by your miscarriage, allow God to come alive in the broken places of your heart. Allow your mind to be transformed by truth. And ask him to integrate the two. He will. He does.

eight

An Invitation to Liberation

There's nothing like a good beating in the waves to make you realize you need a better-fitting bathing suit.

Last summer my family and I were camping at the beach—reconnecting without the internet, deadlines, inboxes, or the ongoing pressures of decision-making. Camping may or may not be your thing, but it most definitely is *ours*.

Going into this trip I had one item at the top of my agenda: Get wet. Swim more. Enjoy the waves. Let the salt water wash my tired body and rejuvenate my soul.

I'm not particularly good at bodysurfing, and I've already told you about my limited brushes with surfing, but I know basic ocean safety and tend to be a decent judge of the scale of an incoming wave—will I jump over it? Or dive under it? I usually make the right call.

Not always.

Every once in a while I decide to jump when I really should have gone under. (Classic rookie mistake.) Of course, when you misjudge a wave it's easy to get tossed around. The force is no small thing. Although I had known for some time I needed to revisit the

101

swimsuit issue after wearing the same one through several pregnant and postpartum beach days over a number of years, one particular crash and the ensuing bathing-suit blunder helped solidify that it was past time to go shopping for a better-fitting suit. Yikes.

And isn't life like that at times? We can know an issue exists, but until it's—ahem—exposed, we do nothing to address it.

The Fruit of Something Deeper

When a friend of mine experienced stillbirth a few months after my first miscarriage, it forced me to look into the eyes of my own jealousy.

Yes, I just said that.

I was devastated to hear her news. It triggered all of my own deep feelings of loss while *also* sending my empathy into overdrive, knowing (on some level) the cauldron of emotions she must have been thrust into.

I did my best to support her (long distance) through emails and responding to her and her family members who immediately turned to me for suggestions for grief support. I gladly did what I could, and it felt good to say "me too" and have something tangible to offer, even if it was simply a list of websites and grief forums that she could check out. But then I watched (via social media) her post professional photos taken with their baby, hold a memorial service at their church, and write of her freezer filled with enough meals to last them weeks. It was beautiful to see how her people rallied, but it also magnified my own lack and amplified all the things I *imagined* would have helped me grieve my own loss.

We didn't have any photos.

We didn't have a grave to visit.

We didn't have a fridge full of food or a mailbox full of cards.

Seeing all that she had in her grief exposed how I felt about what I didn't have. In short, I was jealous. The wave pummeled me and left me naked. My humanity was exposed by something beyond me. As humiliating as it is to have your heart exposed (or your bare bum!), it teaches you something. In this case, it taught more than the fact that I needed new swimmers; it taught me that I needed a renewed heart.

I wouldn't have wished that pain on my friend in a thousand years, and I am so glad she was cared for the way she was. My jealousy had very little to do with her; it had everything to do with my own broken heart.

My jealousy was the fruit of something deeper. It revealed my desire to find comfort in people rather than God. It exposed my sense of entitlement—to be treated the way I thought I would treat others had the tables been turned. It revealed that even though I *knew* what was best for my heart, I didn't always live into it.

Ouch.

While I worked through the issues in my own heart before the Lord, I had to take some tangible steps to make it easier for me: I hid her photos from my Facebook newsfeed, and whenever I began to find myself comparing my pain to her pain or my community's response to her community's response, I began to confess my jealousy to the Lord and use it as a reminder to pray for *her* heart. I don't want to sound trite here, like you can "fix" your heart with a few simple steps. This process wasn't easy for me, but it *was* life-giving. By allowing that specific trigger to become a reminder to lift my gaze to Jesus, I was able to not only support my friend in prayer but make room for God to heal my own heart. (By the way, we're going to delve further into the issue of comparison in the next chapter.)

The Brutal Truth

Grief exposes everything. It exposes our insecurities, our bias, our misdirected beliefs, our weaknesses, our sense of entitlement, our assumptions, our jealousy, our pride. Don't berate yourself for the ugly stuff it uncovers. The human heart is complex—a living, breathing, evolving center of your soul. You can't heal it yourself by applying a spiritual antidote or by white-knuckling your way out of the pain by the power of your will. This is the stuff of spiritual transformation, a partnership between the human and divine. When these things are exposed in our lives, it presents us with an opportunity: Will we allow our weaknesses, sin, and beliefs to define our lives, our faith, and our relationships? Or will we recognize the chance to go deep and deal with the root of our muck?

Now listen, I'm not talking about rolling up your sleeves and digging into your mess when the grief is raw and you're in the depths of your sorrow. Some of you are still spinning from the blow of your miscarriage, and right now you simply need permission to make room for the sadness. Don't minimize or try to "overcome" your grief by crowding it out with soul work.

But others will know exactly what I'm talking about—you are ready. There comes a time when the dust settles and we're faced with the full spectrum of what grief has exposed in our hearts. That's when we have to choose: Will we let our pain dictate our heart responses? Or let it heal and enlarge our heart? This is not God's punishment, or even his discipline. This is his kindness nudging us toward repentance so we can be liberated.[1]

Searching for a Win

Theodore Roosevelt famously said that comparison is the thief of joy. In my experience, comparison is also a sneaky thief of peace.

After our challenging and delightful year living in our caravan in other peoples' driveways all over Australia, we moved into the most gorgeous, old, falling-apart boarding house in inner-city Sydney to plant a new missions hub and begin cultivating community. It was a longed-for homecoming and a relief to unpack our bags in a fixer-upper that would house both our family and our fledgling ministry.

What we didn't realize was that the property was riddled with mold.

We ripped up layers of grotty carpets and vinyl flooring, scrubbed down walls with sugar soap, doused every surface in vinegar, muscled our way through decades of old paint, and only then layered on fresh coats of mold-resistant paint to make it all look pretty and new. We knew it wasn't enough to simply paint over the old stuff, so we took the time to work long, exhausting days for months on end to address the problem in the best way we knew how. We were satisfied, believing we had done a thorough job.

On cold days we could feel a sense of the damp—there were little signs here and there that it wasn't wholly eradicated—but it wasn't until the late summer rains came that we realized the true extent of the problem. The mold was still there, invisible, woven through the innermost parts of our walls, and with each day void of sun the smell of damp made it more and more obvious that our house was still entrenched with mold. The spores were already there, but the damp caused them to breed.

Comparison works like that too. Just as my husband and I had worked hard to address the problem, so I thought I had addressed my problem with comparison when I dealt with the jealousy I felt toward my friend. However, not long after, another situation came up that caused me to examine my heart all over again. And then another. And another.

Reining in a heart prone to comparison is not a "one and done" event but rather an ongoing outworking of the Spirit's movement in our lives, one opportunity at a time.

We might *know* our tendency to compare our lives to others (our loss, problems, circumstances, jobs, joys, family, and any number of things), but most of the time that tendency lurks under the surface, not causing us much pain or disturbance. And then something triggers its reappearance, making it obvious all over again.

Don't be discouraged if this happens to you too. It's part of the process of healing. With each layer of comparison revealed (and the junk that comes with it), God offers an invitation to go deeper. He wants you healed more completely. He wants to set your heart free.

Whose Grief Is Worse, Anyway?

Okay. I have to ask this: Do you hear my story—three miscarriages—and think I have more reason to grieve than you? I remember reading a story after my first miscarriage about a woman who had experienced five. *I could never handle that,* I thought to myself. Subconscious as it was, I believed her grief to be in a different realm than mine. I thought of it like a math equation: She had five times the amount of grief as me. I pitied her and felt foolish for feeling like my world was falling apart even though I had only experienced "one fifth" of what she had. Surely her pain was much worse than mine. And not just worse but *five times worse.*

Or perhaps you hear my story and think I have *less* reason to grieve than you because I easily got pregnant or because I already had living children. Maybe your pregnancy loss came after years of needles and tests and marks on the calendar.

We could play out a dozen scenarios, and they would all land in the same place: Comparison doesn't satisfy. It causes our hearts to be anxious as we question our "right" to feel the way we do. It invites jealousy, resentment, shame, entitlement, and self-pity. It steals peace and circumvents joy. Like the mold problem in our old house, it seeps into the walls of our soul and comes out as soon as it rains; as soon as we're feeling weak or let our guard down, those spores multiply and clog up our airways. We get stuck.

"It's like we're searching for a win," my friend Jess said as we discussed the ills of comparison.

When you feel so awful, it's easy to flail around looking for something to make you feel better. *My loss is more worthy of grief.* Win. *My loss isn't as bad as hers.* Win. *My loss is more tangible, therefore my grief makes more sense.* Win. *My loss is less tangible, therefore my grief hurts more.* Win.

A Temporary Boost

Maybe a "win" like this will leave us temporarily feeling a boost, but ultimately it does nothing to address the interior of our hearts. When Ryan and I discovered the magnitude of the mold problem in our house, we realized our months of hard work weren't enough. The outside brickwork needed to be resealed for moisture, and we needed professional-grade fans installed under the house to aid in circulation. Comparing types of loss (or responses toward loss) is like scrubbing the walls. It may give us a little temporary feeling of "win" but it's short-lived. We must go deeper.

What is it in the human heart that tries to compartmentalize our grief and size it up next to another's? Will it *actually* validate our pain? Will it minimize it? Elevate it? Heal it?

Listen. There will always be someone you think deserves to grieve more than you do. There will always be someone you think deserves to grieve less. But one grief cannot be measured against another. It's your burden to bear. It hurts. Putting it in a lineup will do nothing to heal your soul. Either you will feel justified in your grief and exasperated that others don't see it like you do, or you will berate yourself because your grief feels foolish. Both of these responses are utterly unproductive. (Ask me how I know.)

We must have the courage to feel our pain without exploiting someone else's to make us feel better. We must not allow someone's external responses to their loss dictate the internal responses to our own. The heart needs attending without qualifying statements like, "I know she has it worse than me, but . . ."

Guilty as Charged

Not long after losing Scarlett, I shared with a friend how I thought having living children before my miscarriage made the grief worse than if I had miscarried before carrying a baby to term. My miscarriage was harder, I reasoned, because I understood the magnitude of what I was losing. I felt safe sharing this with her because she, too, had experienced miscarriage after having living children. Clearly I was searching for validation for my pain.

Recalling this conversation now makes me want to facepalm my old self—how untrue and insensitive! In reality, the woman with no living children who miscarries has a whole other grief unfamiliar to me: the grief of being an invisible mother that society doesn't recognize. Who am I to minimize her pain?

Comparison always does this—it makes a mockery of our pain and robs people of dignity while suffering. Comparison tries to boss us into believing we would feel better if only *fill-in-the-blank*, but it's a liar.

You might be comparing your loss to someone else's. *If only I had miscarried earlier, it would hurt less. If only I had been further along and had a chance to hold my baby, I would feel more justified in my pain. If only I knew I could carry to full term, I would have more hope. If only it wasn't so hard for us to get pregnant in the first place, I wouldn't feel so helpless.*

Maybe you're comparing your grief response to a friend's. *She's grieving less; she's probably repressing her grief. She's grieving more; why don't I feel more sadness?*

Perhaps you're comparing your grief to your husband's. *If only he would cry, it would make me feel like he cared. He must not care as much as I do.*

You might be comparing your faith to someone you follow on social media. *If only I had a "strong" faith like hers this would be easier.* (When we pause to think this one through, we see how absurd it is. Only God knows what's going on in the quiet of her heart.)

If only, if only, if only . . .

These comparisons will leave you empty. My guess is you already know exactly what I'm talking about. If you do, you are normal. But you have the power to change. You can—and must—shift your gaze.

Look Instead to Jesus

Let your loss be your loss. Let your grief be your grief. Resist the impulse to search for a temporary win.

I realize how difficult it can be to avoid the sting of someone's joy taking the shape of your pain, or how tempting it can be to find your "win" by comparison to someone else's loss, but as you shift your gaze to Jesus, his kindness will woo you into changing those self-destructive (and relationally destructive) tendencies. The kindness of God is the very best way to turn around a human heart.[2] Let your heart be liberated by responding to his goodness.

When you spend your time looking at and comparing to others, it's impossible to be looking at Jesus. You can't look two directions at once. And when your eyes are off Jesus, it's impossible to see his goodness. We find what we look for, so look to Jesus, dear heart, and let your belovedness inform the way you relate to others.

nine

Thistle Cove

One of the upsides to our year of living in a tiny house on wheels is that we could pack up and leave the place we associated with our pain.

We drove the long way home across Australia after losing our third baby, Ruby, in Perth. It was autumn and still warm enough for us to be enticed to the beach. Thistle Cove seemed like a fitting place to release our goodbyes. There's nothing romantic or warm and fuzzy about thistles, and they spring up in places you wish they wouldn't, but even there among the thistles was an ocean of beauty.

The cove itself was brilliant—clear turquoise waters and frosty white beaches fit for a calendar spread. We found beauty where it shouldn't have been. It seemed the more we experienced pain with our eyes wide open, the more we noticed beauty was amplified too. Somehow it's always there in these ugly-beautiful places, dependent only on our willingness to see.

We released balloons scrawled with messages of farewell and sat on the shore with our sadness for a while. And then, as our hearts settled into another layer of acceptance, we stripped to our undies and went for a spontaneous swim in the deserted cove. *As you do.*

Relationships after loss can feel a bit like Thistle Cove: ugly and beautiful. They hurt and they help. Sometimes you feel deserted, while other times you are spontaneously healed in their embrace.

When You Feel Forgotten

A few days after my second miscarriage that started in Italy and finished in Oregon, I wrote this in my journal:

> *When we announced this pregnancy we had over 700 likes and comments and messages of celebration. The world loves a baby! We love a happy twist after a hard slog—a "rainbow baby," they call it! But where are those people now that we're hurting? Buried under schedules and screens? We have no idea how to enter into one another's pain and so we don't. We whisper, "Oh God, help them! Comfort them!" And these prayers are good and right, yes, but when do we start answering those prayers? When do we start being the help and comfort that we pray for? I went to church this weekend, and as soon as I walked in the door I was confronted all over again with all the people who didn't show up. To make me feel even worse, not a single person acknowledged our miscarriage. I left as alone as when I walked in.*

Clearly an angry, hurting person wrote that journal entry, and I can see now that some of the things I wrote weren't fair, but this is how my grief *felt.* Ryan's too. We felt abandoned and disillusioned. Betrayed, even. It was heartbreak upon heartbreak.

We offered our crushed expectations to the Lord and sensed his grace to forgive. It still hurt, but we knew we'd give bitterness the upper hand and wind up hurting even more if we didn't commit to actively walking in forgiveness. We also knew it wasn't fair of us to presume why people didn't show up like we thought they would. As hard as it was, we couldn't let our feelings be the judge and jury.

Still, we needed our faith in humanity to be repaired.

This Is What the Gospel Looks Like

The following year, when we lost Ruby, the way our friends rallied was so restorative. Even though we were only visiting Perth for a few weeks, I had lived there before marrying Ryan and still had a remnant of dear friends who not only loved us deeply but demonstrated it. The way they loved us through our shock and pain felt like redemption, like a glimpse of heaven.

Also during that time, other friends invited us to come and rest and heal with them, so we detoured south after Thistle Cove before driving back home to Sydney, on the other side of Australia.

We spent more than a week together in their home, and all we did was receive their love. They tended to our hearts as they tended to our bellies. They bought us gifts, pampered us, and created space for us to breathe. They prayed for us. They loved our kids. The women took me to get my hair done and out to eat at a posh restaurant; the men took Ryan to the pub for steak and beers and then out to watch football. They cried with us and laughed with us and prayed with us and sang worship songs over us. This is what the gospel looks like, Ryan and I agreed, these Jesus-people with real hands holding us.

To mourn when others mourn and rejoice when others rejoice is the hard way, but it's the Jesus way.[1] We're learning how to walk in his way together.

But life gets busy, we know. It's easy to think someone else is caring for those who are suffering, we know. It's easy to feel inadequate to care for broken people, we know. Ryan and I have felt all of those things at times—we are guilty of letting our friends and loved ones down. We prayed a lot in those tender days of grief that we wouldn't lose the sense of urgency to care for others when it was our turn to tend to the brokenhearted. We prayed God's grace would help us become friends like our friends had been to us after we lost Ruby.

You see, the truth is, people will hurt you when you are grieving because you're *already* hurt. Grief is just hard. But you can be restored by people too. Community, especially our church communities, can wound us deeply but can heal us even deeper still. God himself is relationship—the Triune God—and as his image bearers, we are created to be in relationship too.

The Cloud of Witnesses

Years ago I heard YWAM[2] Bible teacher Maureen Menard preach on the body of Christ, and she gave the most simple yet profound visual presentation by asking four people to come up to the front. The first three she named "Father," "Son," and "Holy Spirit," and asked them to link arms, representing the perfect communion of the Trinity. She dragged them around the stage to show that wherever the Holy Spirit was, Jesus was too. And wherever Jesus was, so was the Father. And wherever the Father was, so was the Spirit. They do not exist as separate from one another; they're united in perfect relationship.

Then she invited the fourth person to stand inside this little Trinity circle. She described the position of believers as being *in him* and had them walk around the room, tripping on each other, giggling, to show how we can't ever escape the love of God. (God *is* love, remember? And we exist in him.[3])

But then she told us the illustration doesn't stop there. She asked us to imagine the entire congregation within the circle as well. (Thankfully, she didn't ask us all to literally squish in.) As we began to imagine ourselves in that divine circle, in community with one another, she interjected to instruct us to now imagine *all* the saints—past, present, and future—in the circle. All in community with each other and with the perfect community of the Triune God. Remarkable.

It's hard to wrap our brains around this kind of sacred community that encompasses believers throughout the ages. In our individualistic Western society we have an epidemic of me-centered Christianity. (All you have to do is listen to the songs we sing on Sunday mornings to see that they are almost all centered around *me* and *my* relationship with God.) But this was never meant to be the core anchor of our faith. God came to save a people (the nation of Israel) so that all people (*all*—plural!) could be saved through them. God didn't come to save or redeem *me*. He came for *us*.

At the very core of our being we are wired for relationship with him and with each other. Mourning was never meant to be done alone. Rejoicing was never meant to be done alone. Even *salvation* was never meant to be done alone—he came for the *world*.[4]

But we get this wrong, friends. We just do. I do. You do. Your friends do. Your family members do. Usually, we don't mean to. Grief and loss and pain are hard and confusing and uncomfortable. We're clumsy and we mess up community over and over again, but that doesn't mean we can give up on it. *Please don't give up.*

To you whose village didn't show up: I can relate.

To you who've been the recipient of insensitive comments: I can relate.

To you who've felt misunderstood: I can relate.

To you who've been hurt deeply by relationships while you're already grieving: I can relate.

The ache is real, and I'm so sorry you've been wounded. I want to stand in the place of every person who has inflicted more pain in your grief—intentionally or unintentionally—and ask forgiveness on their behalf. I wish I could!

But consider this, friend: *Jesus* can relate. His village abandoned him. He was the recipient of insensitive comments. He was misunderstood. He suffered deep wounding in the midst of his own loss. And at the height of his agony, Jesus said this: "Father, forgive them, for they know not what they do" (Luke 23:34 ESV).

Forgive them. They have no idea.

When Words Wound

In between my first and second miscarriages, I sat around a table eating burgers with several others discussing the day's sessions after a small conference we attended. The woman across from me ordered a beer. "Thank God I'm not pregnant," she laughed. "I can't imagine anything worse right now." I'm not sure what spurred her comments—maybe an inside joke I wasn't aware of—but what I *was* aware of was the color draining from my cheeks. A year after my miscarriage, I hadn't worked up the courage to try to get pregnant again, but there's nothing I wanted more. Her "harmless" jest was salt in my wound, not put there by her but present nonetheless.

Father, forgive them, for they know not what they do.

> Whenever I'm asked how many children I have, I almost always say "two" but what I really want to say is "five." People have no idea how painful this simple question can be. I've answered honestly a few times, but then people usually get super uncomfortable. I have to choose between making others feel awkward or being awkward myself. Either way, it hurts.—Jessica

> The day I shared about my miscarriage on social media I had someone comment that I should "just adopt," as if my miscarriage was like going to the store only to discover they were out of the color shoes I hoped to buy. It was so insensitive. Adoption is a huge deal, and although we would consider it, the suggestion (and its timing) was completely inappropriate.—Lori

People often say things like, "I'm so glad you finally got your baby" now that I have a newborn. I know what they mean, but I guess they have no idea how offensive it is as they imply she is a replacement for the baby I lost.—Dominka

The worst is when friends ask me when we'll start trying again. They have no idea we've already been trying for almost a year. We grieve all over again each month that goes by with no positive pregnancy test. I just wish people would consider their questions a little more.—Tessa

My mother-in-law refuses to acknowledge my miscarriage, because in her mind it wasn't a real baby yet. She even asked me to stop mentioning it publicly because it was embarrassing her to see me "stuck" in my grief in front of her friends.—Anonymous

After my miscarriage, I asked my husband to take a few days off of work to drive me to medical appointments and just to be with me for comfort. His boss refused to give him sick days or bereavement days and said he needed to take his vacation time or work over the weekend instead. It hurts when people don't recognize miscarriage as the loss of a real person.—Tabitha

When I told my best friend we had lost the baby, she said she knew how we felt and then proceeded to talk about how upset she was when her cat died. I understand losing a pet can be awful, but the timing and comparison was so inappropriate. This little child was a person I expected to far outlive me. I had imagined living my whole life as his mother and, if I was lucky, as a grandmother to his children. I know my friend was trying to relate, but she really hurt me in the process.—Racheal

I declined to attend a baby shower for a friend the week after my miscarriage, and sent a gift along with another friend instead. I felt bad, but I didn't think I would be able to hold it together and was afraid of crying all the way through it. She texted me later to accuse me of making her big day about myself. It was awful.—Tiffany

Father, forgive them, for they know not what they do.

We can let these types of encounters cause us to reel in indignation, or we can realize they help illuminate one of the deepest problems surrounding miscarriage: We generally don't know how to respond when people around us are suffering. Perhaps the response is made even more difficult when the suffering comes from a loss that feels abstract to others, such as miscarriage.

I believe part of the reason we find it hard to know how to cope with this type of loss, much less relate to bereaved parents, is because it's so rarely talked about except behind closed doors. In an age where new parents are born into a world of compulsive confession and social sharing, the silence surrounding miscarriage is deafening. Parents of the social media age, who generally feel free to share whatever they'd like, suddenly feel like they've got to keep secrets. Gone is the unmitigated permission to share their parenting journey and in its place is silence and abandonment—perceived or real—that can feel debilitating and isolating. No one talks about it. Or if they do, it's often with a timid "me too" or "I can relate; let's talk privately."

Now please hear me correctly: I'm not saying it's wrong to be private about miscarriage and loss, but what I do want to point out is the perpetual *hush* surrounding miscarriage also creates a perpetual secret grief. Grief left in secret isn't given the opportunity to breathe, receive, and heal in the presence of hopeful, supportive, loving community.

> I had a miscarriage almost fifty years ago when I was five months along. One week I was at church obviously pregnant, the next I was obviously not. No one ever said a word. It's just the way things were back then. All these years later, I've begun to let my heart go there again. Strangely, it feels good to feel the grief. It's lifting the burden, even. I'm glad young people are starting to talk about these things more freely. There's nothing to be ashamed of and we need each other's support when we're hurting.—Alice

I have faith that things are rapidly changing, thanks, in part, to our digital age and the emerging culture influenced by social sharing, and I hope this part of the conversation surrounding miscarriage will be obsolete by the time my children become parents. But for now we're still grasping for a new cultural blueprint to inform the grieving process after miscarriage and other types of pregnancy and baby loss. The culture is still shifting; the stigma is still lifting.

While the cultural conversation is still so new, we can continue to expect awkward and painful encounters. Unfortunately, you and I might never be on the receiving end of an apology from the ones who cause us pain while we grieve, but if we follow the way of Jesus, that pain doesn't have to consume us.

Will you forgive? Will you let go of those unmet expectations? Will you accept that you only see a slice of the story and can never know what your friend or family member went through as they watched you grieve? Will you choose instead to believe they did the best they knew how? Or that even if they didn't, it's not a reflection of how much you are loved and adored and valued by God?

The painful truth is, people rarely know what to say or how to act around those who are suffering and grieving. Death is complicated, especially in cultures where we don't tend to make room for expressions of grief and lament. The intangible death of an unborn baby is that much more complicated because it feels so abstract to most people unless they're right up close.

With all this potential for heartache, you might wonder why it's worth opening up to others at all, but I'm telling you *it's worth it*. This ugly-beautiful mess of community is all we've got, and I wholeheartedly believe the world tips toward beautiful because it's made up of people created in God's beautiful image.

Community can hurt, but it can heal even deeper. Don't let the thistles scare you away, or you'll miss out on something powerful.

Opening up to others and allowing them to respond in love will not only help you but change our future. One small conversation at a time, we are shifting culture in an area where we need to grow—where even the *church* needs to grow: the ability to love and be loved through all of life's seasons. In rejoicing and mourning, in life and death, humans were created for connection.

Let Forgiveness Change Your Future

Before I close this chapter, I want to ask you to invite the Holy Spirit to examine your heart while you consider a few tough questions.

1) Is there anyone you need to forgive?

If we're going to grieve with hope, then we need to grieve in community. I know you may feel weak. I know you may feel vulnerable. But can you give your broken heart to Jesus one more time? Can you release this pain to him? Can you grant forgiveness to those who have hurt you even if they *never even know* they caused a wound? Can you forgive your best friend? Your husband? Your mom who shrugged it off? The doctor who used insulting terminology? The acquaintance who made an insensitive remark? Your boss who didn't give you time off to recover? Your pastor who didn't visit? Your sister who never called?

2) Do *you* need to ask for forgiveness?

Have you been the source of any broken relationships in the wake of your loss? Have you let your sadness cause a wedge between you and a friend? Or let jealousy manifest through harsh words? Have you let your pain justify alienating someone who was trying to help? Have you been quick to judge someone's response (or lack of response) to your grief? Have you resented your husband for grieving differently and let your feelings harm your intimacy? Have you held bitterness toward an unsympathetic family member and started giving them the silent treatment? Have you pushed your living children away? Have you given up on community, on your church, on family, or on friends because they didn't meet your expectations?

3) What about God?

Do you need to ask his forgiveness for the way you assigned blame to him? For assuming he doesn't love you? For accusing him of taking your baby? Or not intervening when he could have? Or believing he doesn't care about your pain?

4) And lastly, friend, do you need to forgive yourself?

I won't qualify this question, but simply place it before you to pick up if you need to.

If you answered *yes* to any of these, I hope you'll realize that part of God mending your broken heart depends on your willingness to forgive and be forgiven. He is absolutely committed to your healing, but there are things he can't do for you. He will never force your hand in order to liberate your heart.

The hard and humble work of forgiveness is always worth it.

Note: If you are reading this book to better understand your friend or loved one's grief, there is a special section at the end of the book for you that delves a bit deeper into how you can care for them while they grieve. Please see appendix E.

Part IV
Invitation

Journal Prompt: Has grief helped expose a need for some soul work so you can be freer to heal? Ask the Holy Spirit if there are issues of shame, guilt, jealousy, comparison, entitlement, or unforgiveness you need to attend to. Have you harbored attitudes or judgments that have shut down God's work of grace for your grief journey? If applicable, write Jesus a letter of confession and invite him to work within your heart in whatever specific areas he shows you. (If nothing specific comes to mind, don't force it.) After you've confessed to Jesus, ask him if there are any relationships you need to mend, and in your own words ask him for humility and the generosity of spirit to be a minister of reconciliation.[5]

Part V

Anchored

A GOD WHO
CAN BE TRUSTED

ten

A Crisis of Faith or a Catalyst for Grace?

I know exactly what it feels like to sense God speaking to me in detail about a baby before conception, have the entire thing come true, and then watch the baby die anyway. This happened to me three times. Three intimate stories with detail beyond what most would consider coincidental. Three stories that felt like miracles. All three followed by miscarriage.

Have you ever felt like Jesus led you somewhere and then took off as soon as you got there?

Me too.

Sleeping Jesus

Remember when Jesus and his disciples were on the boat in the storm?[1] The disciples were scared for their lives when the wind and seas turned furious. It must have been a grim outlook for these robust young men to feel so vulnerable and afraid. And then, to their shock and dismay, they found Jesus sleeping through their worst nightmare. This, the guy whose idea it was in the first place.

There he was—present, but asleep. Great.

What did these tough guys do when Jesus wasn't meeting their needs the way they thought he should? They panicked and woke him up, begging for help. (Sound familiar?)

And what did Jesus do? He responded and spoke to the storm, telling it to be still.

Jesus didn't base his response to his disciples on whether or not their panic was warranted or wise; he responded to the fact that they woke him and sought him in their time of need. He responded because of who he is—good, gracious, kind, a man of peace—not because their panic and fear demanded it.

I love this about Jesus, because there have been plenty of times in my own life when I've felt like I needed to shake him awake in my own panic too. Every time I thought the storm would consume me, his grace has sustained me.

In the case of these disciples, his grace looked like calming the seas. We don't always get grace in the shape we hope for, but we always get it in *some* shape when we ask.[2]

Has it seemed as though Jesus is sleeping through *your* storm?

I felt like I had a strong faith before I miscarried, but all of a sudden, my doubts about God became debilitating. I felt totally abandoned, like, where did he go when I needed him most? I had so many questions, which left me feeling like a failure of a Christian.—Jen

Experiencing miscarriage derailed my faith completely. If a loving God would allow this to happen, then I have one thing to say about it: F&#% him. I'm done with Christianity. This feels nothing like love.—Beth

I had no experience with trauma before my miscarriage, and when I tried to combine the belief that God was in control *and* that I had a miscarriage anyway, the wheels started to fall off of my faith. I got totally stuck and began to resent this *supposedly* "good" God, but I didn't feel safe to process my questions with anyone. I felt like if I was honest, my husband and friends would assume I was backsliding.—Anonymous

Friend, you may be anchored to despair or confusion, anger or sorrow. You may be afraid your faith can't hold up to the scrutiny of the doubts or questions your pain has exposed. You may feel caught in a free fall where one question leads to another, and the Sunday school answers you've recited your whole life just aren't working anymore.

Pain, grief, and suffering have a way of unearthing questions and doubts we didn't even realize we had, but that's not a bad thing. When you're in the tender days of a fresh loss, the most important thing you need to know is that Jesus is in the boat with you. It might seem like he took off, but he didn't. He's still there, and he's not going to bail.

Jesus always answers our questions with *presence* first (as we explored in part II), but that doesn't mean we are to disregard them. So grab hold of all of those Big Questions and dive deep. Yup, that's right—bring them with you. Your doubts and questions may frighten you, but they don't intimidate God.

Faith, Doubt, and the Tension Holding Them Together

What do we do when it feels like our faith is thrown up against the rocks and left to bleed there? Miscarriage, like other personal trauma, can be the undoing of our faith if we don't hold space for our doubts and questions amid the anguish and trust that God can meet us there too.

Many of us hold this perception that faith is a force or conviction that is concrete, proven, immovable. We see faith as certainty, the opposite of doubt, and conclude that to have faith means we cannot waiver. The term "woman of faith" conjures up the image of a woman with an iron backbone: She stands attentive and steady in the battle, she's armed with all the right Bible verses, she does not get shaken in the face of adversity, and nothing will be able to penetrate this shield of faith she holds fast to. We minimize the mysteries of the Christian life down to these caricatures and believe doubt is the enemy of faith. *But we're dead wrong.*

In reality, doubt is a part of faith. It's because of doubt (and/or uncertainty) that faith is required in the first place. Most of us don't have faith in gravity, because we're already certain it exists. It takes no guts, no trust, no *faith* to believe that when we jump into a pool we'll actually land in the water and not in the tree overhead.

Similar to courage—which we have no need for unless something frightens or worries us—we have no need for faith unless there's something unknown or unseen, some variable of doubt or uncertainty. Like courage can't exist without fear as a precursor, faith can't exist without something creating the need for it. Doubt precedes the strengthening of our faith—*if* we are willing to engage with it in the presence of Jesus rather than ignore it, run from it, or try to work it out apart from him. Surprisingly, doubt can be a gift (though, admittedly, an uncomfortable one).

What *is* faith, then, if it's not a certainty of beliefs or the absence of doubt? Faith, in the Christian context, is covenant with Jesus. Faith says that I commit myself to him even while not knowing every exhaustive *why* or *how* or *when* of who he is and how he operates. Faith is a gift we are given and a gift we give, both.

When I vowed "I do" to my husband, I did so in faith. I couldn't be certain of every decision he'd ever make, or career changes he'd undergo, or habits he'd form, or what slips of character or victories or failures he'd have. Yet still, I made the covenant. Faith is saying *yes* to him because I've committed to give the marriage everything I've got, believing my covenant promise is the best possible way to grow in the relationship. Faith is risky because it leans into that which is yet unknown and says "I do" anyway.

Faith with God can feel risky too. How can we ever know the depth of his ways? How can we ever know the extent of his thoughts? How can we be certain the whole thing isn't a sham? We can't. Not entirely. But faith says *yes* anyway. Faith makes a covenant to fall forward into trust, believing that God has given us every reason to hope in his goodness, starting with what he's already done for us.

"Faith shows the reality of what we hope for; it is the evidence of things we cannot see" (Heb. 11:1). If all of the unseen could be seen (or touched, felt, heard, and so on), then it simply wouldn't be faith. Our faith in Jesus is our covenant to give our lives to him, regardless of the mystery—*that* is the hallmark of an exquisite and authentic faith, not the absence of doubt or an encyclopedia-sized brain full of memory verses. Faith is all the stuff we're uncertain about but put our hope in anyway, because we believe God is who he says he is.

Who Is This God?

The best news for you and me is that we can confidently place our hope (the stuff we can't yet see) in God—a Jesus-looking God with a Jesus-looking ministry.

We didn't hear the term until several years later, but it was during the months of grappling with Judah's prognosis during my second pregnancy that Ryan and I grew in our understanding of the theology of a "Jesus-looking God," as coined by pastor-theologian Greg Boyd. Colossians 1:15 says that Jesus came as the exact representation of God the Father and, therefore, what we see in Jesus is exactly the same stuff that God the Father is made of. Jesus is the clearest picture of God (Father, Son, Holy Spirit) we have.[3]

This revelation of *God as seen in Jesus* is the best news the world has ever heard. If Jesus came to show us the Father and to begin the process of making all things new, he brought with him an understanding of God that liberates tremendous hope, assurance, and peace. Our faith—doubts and all—is the substance of things hoped for.

When Jesus walked the earth he filled his days with people most would have overlooked: prostitutes, liars, thieves, smelly fishermen, budding-but-immature pastors and wannabe theologians, widows, lepers, the mentally ill, demoniacs, the sick, and the dying. His constant ministry was bringing life and healing to dead and wounded souls and bodies. He was the kind of God who was interruptible, the kind of God who noticed pain and doubts and suffering and confusion, the kind of God who engaged deeply with people so that his heart would be *moved* to take action when they needed him most.

He was a healer who didn't stop at incomplete healing. "I can see men as trees!" the blind man rejoiced after Jesus healed him (Mark 8:24 KJV). But "men as trees" was not good enough. Jesus kept ministering, kept releasing the healing power of God until the man's vision was restored with clarity and completeness (v. 25). With Jesus, our hope is complete.

Does your faith feel blurry, like "men as trees"? Tell him! Tell him you can't see clearly. Jesus will meet you there; he doesn't stop birthing life into dead places. He has been healing you and is *still* healing you. He's not finished!

We can place our hope in ten thousand things. When you're in the thick of grieving, it's easy to place your hope in finding answers, in statistics and science, in the comfort of others, or even in the validation of your pain. Perhaps, for some of us, we'd like to place our hope in tidy theology, having all of our questions and confusion about God summed up and resolved in easily digested sound bites. Although all of those things can be good and helpful, the only *sure* thing we can put our hope in is Jesus Christ himself.

Friend, putting your hope in Jesus is not a cliché. We have to swallow that truth, hard. Putting our hope in Jesus is work; it's intentional and it's worth it. It means acting on the covenant of faith ("Yes, I choose you, God") and leaning in to who he is—not only our experience of who we believe him to be but who *he* says he is and who *he* demonstrates himself to be in scripture.

Hope is bound up tightly with trust, and we must believe it's possible to trust him even while holding our doubts and unknowns before him.

A God We Can Hope in; a God We Can Trust

What do you tell your four-year-old when he should be snuggled up in bed but instead he's asking why Jesus didn't bring our own baby back to life like he did with Lazarus?[4] *Because can't Jesus do that?*

"I don't know, baby. I don't know."

That's what I told Levi, because I *don't know* why he doesn't bring our babies back to life.

"But do you think God can still be good, even if we don't know?" I continued. "Do you think we can still trust him? What do you think, baby?"

Yes, he nodded. And I was glad. "But mom, I'm not a baby," he said. "I'm a big boy."

Indeed, son. A big boy with a big heart.

If there's one thing I want to teach my children (and hold fast to myself), in the midst of all the pain and injustice, suffering and heartache I see around me, it's that God is unequivocally good. Everything around us might falter or change or disappear, but his goodness has always been and will be. This kind of goodness doesn't order pain, doesn't "allow" evil, doesn't direct punishment to teach us a lesson—not here, not now. This God of ours isn't cruel or disconnected or self-righteous or proud.

This God—our Jesus—is humble and long-suffering and load-bearing and loving. Along with us, he is weeping and mourning, feasting and rejoicing through it all. He loves at all costs, even to the point of giving us total and complete freedom to reject all that is good and pure and exchange it for evil. (We'll examine this more deeply in the next chapter.) He's always stood on the side of the marginalized, the outcast, the *hurting*—you and I. He is *for* us.

Jesus is the one who embodies compassion, kindness, love, and goodness. He is the one who offers the grace we need to make it through our darkest nights. We can let our tragedy propel us into a crisis of faith, or we can redirect it to become a catalyst for God's grace to do the deep work of *growing* our faith. As hard as it is, the choice is ours.

In 2 Corinthians 12:9, the apostle Paul describes God's grace as being "sufficient" (ESV). The Greek word for this is *arkeó*, and it means "enough."[5] It is a present tense verb, meaning it's constantly available. Do you know what this means, friends? It means that God's grace is cut to measure for us—right here, right now—for our exact set of circumstances. He doesn't "over-grace" us, and he will never, ever "under-grace" us. This is some of the best news I've ever heard.

When I began to ask the inevitable "Why, God?" questions after Judah's prognosis, again after Scarlett's death, again through our struggle to conceive after losing her, again after losing Oliver, again after losing Ruby, and again during my pregnancy with our youngest son, Micah (my hardest pregnancy of all of them), God's grace was there for me in precisely the measure I needed. It always is, but we have to learn how to recognize and receive it.

There is grace for the question-asking. There is grace for the duck-and-weave through doubt. There is grace for the "faintest yes" and the full-volume angry shout. There is grace present in the boat, even when it seems Jesus is sleeping. There is grace for it all.

Accessing the Grace

I brought to my grief decades' worth of life experiences that helped shape my view of God's character and ways. Whether consciously or unconsciously, you do the same. It would be naive of us to think that you and I would arrive at the same place while on such different paths. I'm not here to spoon-feed you theology, but I will ask you this: Will you turn to Jesus? Will you believe he's in the boat even when the storm is still raging? Will you let him use your pain—your own personal Scarlett—to show you his grace? Rather than trying to climb out of your grief or wondering when God will rescue you, will you be bold enough to ask him to remake you?

Look your doubt in the eye and whisper, "Welcome. Show me how to take my faith deeper."

Offer Jesus your questions. Offer him your doubts. Offer him your fears. Offer him your anxiety, your anger, your depression, your despair. Offer him your confusion, your numbness, your shock, your sadness. Offer him your longing. Offer him your dreams—the broken ones and the ones still intact.

As hard as it is to examine our beliefs, pain can help us get desperate enough to do it. So offer him yourself, beloved. Let your crisis of faith become a catalyst for grace.

He is not offended by our lack of certainty over the Big Questions; he'll never equate our doubts or confusion with a lack of faith if, while questioning, we stay committed to relationship with him. This is why covenant matters. Your belonging to him, and his belonging to you—it matters.

God will not shy away from your messy faith or your messy theology or your messy life. He will not despise your brokenness. He will not be threatened by your doubts, or even your accusations—as unfair as they might sometimes be. If your doubt is debilitating, release your questions to him and to someone close to you whom you trust with your heart who will listen and pray for you and encourage you to keep on questioning as long as you need to. Your questions aren't a detour; they're the way forward.

Although *you* might be, God is not afraid of you losing your religion; he only wants to keep your heart.

> Keep on asking, and you will receive what you ask for. Keep on seeking, and you will find. Keep on knocking, and the door will be opened to you. (Matt. 7:7)

eleven

Whose Fault Is This, Anyway?

*F*rom the beginning of time, humankind has grappled with the question of God's intent in times of crisis. Does he inflict suffering? Allow it? Endorse it? Order it to teach us a lesson? Mandate it to mature us in our faith? Ignore it?

More than the questions about the biology of reproduction, our bodies, medical procedures, or even how to process grief, how to share the news with friends and family, or how to know if what we're feeling is normal, the questions tangled up in our faith can be the most debilitating.

Have you ever found yourself asking God something like this?

"Why would you let this happen?"

"Don't you care about me?"

"Why didn't you save my baby?"

"Why would you give me a baby and then take him away?"

Perhaps you've wrestled with similar questions. Or perhaps you've kept them under lock and key because you felt like whispering them aloud would be akin to admitting you're unsure of God's goodness or his love. Maybe you're afraid your faith isn't as strong as it "should" be.

While I won't spend chapters unpacking the issue of *Is God to blame for our suffering?* (though I do list resources for further study in appendix F), I would be remiss not to address this elephant of a question, squished here into the room we share.

He Gives and Takes Away—Are You Sure?

If you have pointed questions and loaded conclusions about God's involvement in your suffering, you aren't alone.

Listen to Naomi:

> Things are far more bitter for me than for you, because the LORD himself has raised his fist against me. (Ruth 1:13)

> "Don't call me Naomi," she responded. "Instead, call me Mara,[1] for the Almighty has made life very bitter for me. I went away full, but the LORD has brought me home empty. Why call me Naomi when the LORD has caused me to suffer and the Almighty has sent such tragedy upon me?" (vv. 20–21)

Job might set the gold standard for the tough questions and pointed accusations he leveled at God (not surprisingly, considering all he lost and endured):

> The LORD gave me what I had,
>   and the LORD has taken it away.
> Praise the name of the LORD! (Job 1:21)

> I am innocent,
>   but it makes no difference to me—
>   I despise my life.
> Innocent or wicked, it is all the same to God.
>   That's why I say, "He destroys both the blameless and
>   the wicked."

When a plague sweeps through,
   he laughs at the death of the innocent.
The whole earth is in the hands of the wicked,
   and God blinds the eyes of the judges.
   If he's not the one who does it, who is? (9:21–24)

I was living quietly until he shattered me.
   He took me by the neck and broke me in pieces. . . .
Again and again he smashes against me,
   charging at me like a warrior. (16:12, 14)

I cry to you, O God, but you don't answer.
   I stand before you, but you don't even look.
You have become cruel toward me.
   You use your power to persecute me.
You throw me into the whirlwind
   and destroy me in the storm. (30:20–22)

Throughout the centuries, Christians have praised the psalmists for their emotional honesty. Listen to a few examples from the psalms. David said:

O LORD, how long will you forget me? Forever?
   How long will you look the other way?
How long must I struggle with anguish in my soul,
   with sorrow in my heart every day? (Ps. 13:1–2)

In Psalm 44 the descendants of Korah let loose a barrage of accusations, accusing God of tossing them aside (v. 9), butchering them like sheep (v. 11), and covering them with darkness and death (v. 19). The psalm then continues:

Wake up, O Lord! Why do you sleep?
   Get up! Do not reject us forever!
Why do you look the other way?
   Why do you ignore our suffering and oppression?
                (vv. 23–24)

The prophet Habakkuk also takes his turn:

> How long, O LORD, must I call for help?
>> But you do not listen!
> "Violence is everywhere!" I cry,
>> but you do not come to save.
> Must I forever see these evil deeds?
>> Why must I watch all this misery? (Hab. 1:2–3)

Now, to be fair, this is a sampling plucked out of scripture, so we need to remember these are pulled from the stories that give them context. But my point here is to show you we have always questioned God (yes, even the faithful saints who've gone before us, whom we hail as heroes of the faith). Throughout the centuries we have ascribed malicious intent to and cast blame on God when grasping to make sense of the chaos around us. We've wondered why he seems silent and have assumed that meant absent. We've been baffled over why he didn't intervene to heal, deliver, or change a desperate situation. We've felt abandoned, forgotten, and uncared for. We've even accused him of orchestrating (or specifically allowing) some of the very things that have caused us—and dare I say *him*—gut-wrenching pain. (Like our miscarriages?) We've forgotten his job description, which is to give life, and have, at times, credited him with the work of the enemy of our soul, which is to steal, kill, and destroy.[2]

I realize examining these scriptures—and God's role in suffering or how his will and humankind's free will plays out—might feel challenging, perhaps even confrontational. These are not easy theological concepts to grapple with. But as you consider these passages, keep in mind that all of these examples are people who loved and served God. All of them explicitly praise him even in the midst of their suffering. (Paul reminds us of the importance of this in Romans 5:3–6, exhorting us to let pain and suffering become our teacher and to receive God's sacrificial love even there as we learn.) Bear in mind these heroes were also human: They praised *and accused*, sometimes in the same breath.

Even When We're Wrong

Here's something we must seriously consider: What if these accusations we level at God—you're butchering me like a sheep, forgetting me, taking me by the neck and breaking me in pieces, laughing at innocent death, destroying my home and family and livelihood—aren't true? What if they are included in the Bible so we can see the history of God's people in all its gruesome detail? What if God treasures our emotional integrity and willingness to bare our whole selves before him *even when we're wrong*? What if he's confident his kindness can lead us to repentance when we've misjudged him?[3] (We see an amazing example of repentance in Job 42, when Job realizes how wrong he was about God in his earlier accusations about God's role in his demise.)

What if God is trying to demonstrate to us how *normal* it is to feel what we feel, and to let our best questions rip, while also showing us how to proclaim his faithfulness, continue to trust him, and ultimately allow him the space to incarnate himself into our mess and bring about a rebirth from within it? What if the whole Bible is about making broken things whole, answering the problem of suffering with the hope of glory, and exchanging the sorrow of death for abundant life?

What if it's a redemption story after all?

God is in the business of making all things new. *This is always the point.*

He doesn't prescribe pain and suffering for some mysterious greater good, or to teach us a lesson, or to shape us into better versions of ourselves like a mother sneaking broccoli into her child's spaghetti sauce. He is not manipulative and he will never abuse his power. He doesn't exploit our vulnerability or trick us into growth—a bait and switch, swapping bread for stone behind our backs.[4] He takes dead things and makes them alive. He heals wounds. He binds up the darkness. He inspires hope. He gives his life for ours, because that's exactly what love looks like.[5]

Our Honesty Gives Him a Chance to Set the Record Straight

And in case you're still hesitant, here's where I want you to lean in close, sister, and consider the words of one more person from the Bible. Listen to what Jesus cried during his darkest moment:

My God, my God, why have you forsaken me? (Matt. 27:46 ESV)

This word *forsaken* means "abandoned, rejected, despised." We can imagine it said this way: *My God, why have you abandoned me? What did I do to deserve this rejection? Do you despise me? Hate me?*

This, coming from *within* the Trinity, from Jesus to the Father. This, coming from a man intimately acquainted with humanity and divinity, bridging the divide for us all. Yes, even *this* man still leveled with the Father. He spilled out his guts to him before spilling them for us—what trust, what hope, what love he demonstrated!

My point, again, is this: God is not threatened by our difficult, pointed questions. He's not disappointed by our humanity—our doubts, fears, anger, confusion, or despair. He can handle it all, even our accusations, knowing they don't automatically cancel out our belief in, or commitment to, him.

God loves our honesty because it gives him a chance to set the record straight.

As you wade through grief, remember this: Your grief—your emotions, your questions, your mess—none of it is "too much" for God. Like a mother longs to gather her hurting child into her arms, so God wants to gather you into his.[6] He's not offended or surprised by your human response to grief and suffering; he simply wants to be born into it and through it. Your humility to approach him *exactly as you are* releases his grace over your life.[7] He is present to help you.

Writing Purpose into Our Pain

While I don't believe God orchestrates suffering or death, scripture makes it abundantly clear that he can and will employ every means possible to bring about good in our lives from it. Remember Romans 8:28, which we unpacked in chapter 6? "We know that in everything God works for good *with* those who love him, who are called according to his purpose" (Rom. 8:28 RSV, emphasis mine).

He brings about good from any situation *with us*. He didn't take our three babies so we could welcome our youngest son, Micah, into the world, though it's true he wouldn't exist had we not miscarried Scarlett, Oliver, and Ruby. (And obviously we're *profoundly* thankful for Micah's life.) But God doesn't take a life in order to give a life; he's the *author* of life, the *source* of life, the *resurrector* of life. He's a miracle worker, always taking what was intended for evil and turning it around for good. We see this repeated many times throughout the Bible, but chiefly we see it in Jesus himself.

Jesus's crucifixion was a sacrifice of love, but its *origin* was our doing—our sin, our rebellion, our inability to recognize him as the Messiah. And yet even there, among the consequences of humanity's sin, Jesus was working toward God's ultimate, overarching will: the reconciliation of all things, the kingdom of heaven that cannot be thwarted, the new city the apostle John speaks of where there will be no tears and no more suffering in the age to come.[8]

The very thing that was meant to destroy him became our deliverance. *Astounding.*

The suffering of the cross became the pathway to freedom. *Breathtaking.*

The evil and injustice and agony of the crucifixion became our doorway to abundant life. *Staggering.*

His is a story of grace like Scarlett—the stuff of an upside-down kingdom, foolish things confounding the wise, and dead things becoming alive. No mind could comprehend this kind of revolutionary love that would enter something evil and transform it into something powerful enough to redeem the darkest soul—resurrection of the dead, joy from mourning. The crucifixion was never God's original design; it was his redemption plan.

Friend, suffering was not his design for you either, but he'll use it as a pathway for redemption. It's what he does—he makes broken things whole; he makes dead things come alive. God's sovereign promise to us is this: *He has the final word.*

> For I am God, and there is no other;
>   I am God, and there is none like me,
> declaring the end from the beginning
>   and from ancient times things not yet done,
> saying, "My counsel shall stand,
>   and I will accomplish all my purpose."
>   (Isa. 46:9–10 ESV)

Nothing Will Be Wasted

Jesus is in the business of tear-wiping, of making all things new, of lighting up the dark places, and of stomping out death, bringing beauty from ashes, and making broken hearts whole. He will turn your Scarlett into his grace. The gospel is *such* good news.

The truth is, he hasn't forsaken you. He hasn't abandoned you. He's not some cruel taskmaster or sneaky manipulator orchestrating tragedy in your life in order to teach you a lesson or mature your faith. He takes no delight in our suffering, but he *does* promise to fellowship with us there and grow us more into his likeness, embracing the opportunity to teach and mature us. This is God's miraculous ability to write purpose into our pain when it inevitably comes.

Amazing.

So, friend, please don't let false notions of who God is cause you to lose your trust in him. A. W. Tozer said, "What comes into our minds when we think about God is the most important thing about us."[9] Our view of God changes everything. It affects the way we see ourselves, the world, and life itself.

Will you let your hardest questions lead you closer to the Lord? You might feel a sense of injustice that makes you stand and rage, or perhaps you feel a crushing sadness that sends you back to your knees. Whatever you feel, will you let him answer with his goodness and show you what he's really like? You will never make a better investment in your life than time spent discovering who God is. He is beautiful, he is Love, and he can be found.

Part V
Invitation

Journal Prompt: Write a letter to God and include all of your Big Questions. Let 'em rip. Yes, he knows them already, but he longs for the sort of relationship where you hold nothing back from him—total transparency. He wants your whole heart, and this includes your willingness to be vulnerable and be fully known in his presence. Don't sugarcoat your doubts, fears, confusion, or accusations. Like Job, Naomi, and David, get them all out in the open, if you haven't already. Follow the example of Jesus: He asked the Father his anguished question ("Why have you forsaken me?") and then committed his spirit into God's hands.[10] Jesus questioned *and* he trusted—God invites us to do the same.

Part VI

Onward

ADJUSTING YOUR SAILS
FOR UNCHARTED WATERS

twelve

The Business of Tear-Wiping

I'll meet her before you do, you know."

When my grandmother said this to me, it made me blink hard. Maybe I wasn't used to having others refer to our baby in a way that was so concrete, or maybe I was still getting used to hearing her talk candidly about her impending transition from her earthly home to her heavenly home. Either way, her statement caught me with my defenses around my knees.

I may have cried a little as her simple words burned into my memory.

That was nearly four years ago.

During a visit last month, my now ninety-one-year-old grandmother asked, "What was her name again?"

"Who, Grandma?"

"The baby you lost."

Scarlett, Oliver, Ruby. I reminded her of all three.

Grandma's slowing down, finding it hard to get out of bed. Her body causes her grief as she contends with its aches and malfunctions. I can hear hunger in her voice when she talks about heaven. She misses Grandpa. Her eyes hang wistful over a tired smile.

She's ready.

I have thought about heaven more during the last four years than my entire life put together. Even now I try to imagine Grandma being greeted by one of our little ones—or all of them, perhaps. Who knows?

Truthfully, I've never understood heaven and have often been confused by the mixed messages preached from pulpits and espoused in popular Christian fiction. The children's Bible answers and Sunday school lessons have left me wanting. Although I've done my fair share of wrestling through all sorts of theological issues, I have been mostly content to leave heaven in the "mystery" box to be figured out later (or not). But since losing my own babies, this has slowly begun to shift.

I don't know what heaven is like. I suspect it's not much like what most of us imagine. The Bible is full of beautiful imagery and metaphor, and yet so much mystery still surrounds this *other* place or dimension—our true home. The best description (outside of scripture) I've ever considered is one I first heard at eight years old and have read many times since:

> The difference between the old Narnia and the new Narnia was like that. The new one was a deeper country: every rock and flower and blade of grass looked as if it meant more. I can't describe it any better than that: if ever you get there you will know what I mean.
>
> It was the Unicorn who summed up what everyone was feeling. He stamped his right fore-hoof on the ground and neighed, and then he cried:
>
> "I have come home at last! This is my real country! I belong here. This is the land I have been looking for all my life, though I never knew it till now. The reason why we loved the old Narnia is that it sometimes looked a little like this. Bree-hee-hee! Come further up, come further in!"[1]

I imagine that heaven looks a lot like this earth we love, but truer and deeper, and that somehow it will be entirely different and entirely familiar all at the same time. And yes, I admit some of this imagination has been triggered by a child's storybook. But it's also been spurred by the Bible. Consider this passage:

> Look! I am creating new heavens and a new earth,
>> and no one will even think about the old ones anymore.
> Be glad; rejoice forever in my creation!
>> And look! I will create Jerusalem as a place of happiness.
>> Her people will be a source of joy.
> I will rejoice over Jerusalem
>> and delight in my people.
> And the sound of weeping and crying
>> will be heard in it no more.
>
> No longer will babies die when only a few days old.
>> No longer will adults die before they have lived a full
>> life.
> No longer will people be considered old at one hundred!
>> Only the cursed will die that young!
> In those days people will live in the houses they build
>> and eat the fruit of their own vineyards.
> Unlike the past, invaders will not take their houses
>> and confiscate their vineyards.
> For my people will live as long as trees,
>> and my chosen ones will have time to enjoy their hard-
>> won gains.
> They will not work in vain,
>> and their children will not be doomed to misfortune.
> For they are people blessed by the LORD,
>> and their children, too, will be blessed. (Isa. 65:17–23)

A Glorious Hope

As I've begun to learn about the new heaven and the new earth—the renewal of all things—that the Bible describes in both the Old and New Testaments, many (if not most) of my ideas about what heaven is have been found to be flimsy under scrutiny. The absence of white fluffy clouds seems glaring in scripture, and in its place is a whole slew of references to the renewal of all things, beginning with the resurrection of Jesus and culminating with God making his home among his people—here! On earth! As heaven and earth collide and merge and become reborn in Christ![2] (Yes—so many exclamation marks!)

In Matthew 19:28, when Jesus talks about the world being made *new*, the word is sometimes translated as "regeneration." The original language here was the Greek word *paliggenesía*, which literally means "genesis again."[3] This same word is used in Titus to refer to what happens to new believers:

> He saved us, not because of the righteous things we had done, but because of his mercy. He washed away our sins, giving us a new birth and new life through the Holy Spirit. (Titus 3:5)

This regeneration, renewal, or rebirth that Jesus and Paul speak of is for the world and for us—for all creation, heaven and earth.

Of course this isn't the book in which to unpack thousands of years of church tradition, worldview, or eschatology (much more qualified theologians can help you with that—please see the resource section in appendix F). But as we're faced with our present grief, loss exposes an opportunity for us to examine "life after life" as we know it in a way that elicits tremendous hope. N. T. Wright calls this the "after, after life"—our hope in the age to come, which is *more* than simply being in the presence of God, it is seeing the cosmos re-created to its original design.

Honestly? This makes me both extremely uncomfortable (because it reveals how much I have yet to learn) while also leaves me brimming with new, hopeful anticipation. (Isn't life the most grand and curious learning curve?)

While some of these concepts feel so new to me, they also feel familiar. Think about a moment in your life when you felt a taste of heaven on earth: the edge of a cliff overlooking a stunning vista, the declaration of your wedding vows, a wave of transcendent worship during a concert, a quiet stillness by candlelight where you sensed the nearness of the Holy Spirit, the breath of your newborn nephew, the flutter of your heart when you *know* you've just heard a word from the Lord, a phone call from a friend when you wondered if anyone recognized your pain, a feast encircled with laughter and rich wine in Tuscany. These moments feel like heaven on earth because they are—they are the kingdom of heaven breaking into our *now*.

We recognize this "heaven" in Jesus as he spent his whole ministry demonstrating what heaven on earth looks like. Jesus often talked about the kingdom of heaven (or the kingdom of God) as he taught his followers and ministered to others.[4] For you and I, it's probably easiest to imagine the "kingdom" he referred to as an actual location, because our earthly kingdoms have geopolitical boundaries and places. And yet, as I've begun to study scripture more seriously, I've started to see that Jesus was talking about a way of life, not just a place where that life exists. He came to *show* us heaven, not just take us there.

I've spent a great deal of time showcasing Jesus's ministry in previous chapters—always he's demonstrating what the kingdom of heaven looks like: healed bodies, saved souls, freedom from bondage, broken things being made whole, storms calmed, suffering alleviated, religion turned upside down by radical love, union with God. These are all glimpses of heaven breaking into the present. What Jesus made manifest is still happening and will continue to unfold as he heals all of creation.

Am I saying that we don't "go" to be with Jesus when we die? No, I am not. Scripture gives us good reason to believe our babies are in the presence of God—divine Love—even now. The language we use for death fails us; these babies aren't dead, they aren't lost. They are alive and found in him for eternity. We grieve their loss to us here and now, yes, but we grieve *with hope* because we know there is more to the story.

Not only are they with Jesus now but there is more to come—the after, after life—a time when all is made new, the new heaven and the new earth established when Christ returns to set the world right and re-create all things. We won't be strumming harps, bored for an eternity. Like Isaiah 65 says, we'll be planting vineyards and building houses, and our work won't be in vain. Our children will flourish. We will no longer suffer pain. We'll have no reason to weep, no relationship or body broken, no unrealized God-given dreams. God has the final word. He has always been and will always be *for* us.

A Divine Homesickness

Since I've lived overseas from my nation of origin for most of my adult life, I'm accustomed to feeling a bit "other." I'm the one with the accent; I'm the one with the head tilted, wondering why my order of "lemonade" will land me a Sprite on the table. By the time you read these words I will have taken the oath to become Australian, so I won't technically be able to call myself an "alien" anymore, but one thing I've realized in these almost twenty years of foreign post codes is that my passport may be American (or, soon, Australian), but my citizenship is in heaven, and my home is in Jesus.[5]

Our citizenship is lodged somewhere completely *other* (heaven) and also completely *here* (earth). The kingdom of God is at hand, and the kingdom of God is still coming—the paradox of the *now* and *not yet*, the mixed metaphor of roots and wings—our longing to burrow down and our longing to fly—it's Jesus calling us home, reminding us that we're still aliens, exiles, sojourners on the way *there* even as we find ourselves in him *here*. The homesickness of the human heart teaches us to identify the eternity God's buried within.[6]

Maybe that's exactly why we will always hold a hint of feeling like we don't belong—because we don't. Well, not entirely, at least. God has put a taste for heaven in our souls, and when we pause long enough to notice, we can feel it—this thing within that yearns for a home we've never set foot in yet have always been. What lies before us holds more beauty and possibility than the deepest, truest form of earth we can imagine—it's better than Narnia by a thousand times.

The writer of Hebrews calls it a city which is to come;[7] the apostle John gives us just enough vision to leave us dripping with desire:

> Then I saw a new heaven and a new earth, for the first heaven and the first earth had passed away, and the sea was no more. And I saw the holy city, new Jerusalem, coming down out of heaven from God, prepared as a bride adorned for her husband. And I heard a loud voice from the throne saying, "Behold, the dwelling place of God is with man. He will dwell with them, and they will be his people, and God himself will be with them as their God. He will wipe away every tear from their eyes, and death shall be no more, neither shall there be mourning, nor crying, nor pain anymore, for the former things have passed away." (Rev. 21:1–4 ESV)

The picture John paints in Revelation is powerful, because it's not just some new place we'll be whisked away to once we take our last breath on earth. It's much more profound than that. He's painting a picture of a renewed creation—a resurrected, regenerated, *re-created* creation—where heaven and earth collide and there is no relational division between God and humankind. He's speaking of the day in an age to come where "on earth as it is in heaven" is not just a petition for what could be but a declaration of what *is*.

Just like when Paul says God makes us into a "new creation" when we come to faith in Jesus,[8] so heaven and earth will be "born again" (made new) and renewed by the same resurrection power of God that raised Jesus from the dead. The same word for new (*kainos*) is used to describe believers as a new creation in Christ *and* for the new heaven and earth described in Revelation 21, and means *new in quality* or *fresh and unused*.[9]

N. T. Wright has often said that the resurrected Jesus is not only the model for what's to come but also the means in which we get there. Jesus came to show us what being renewed looks like, and in the age to come, all those who are in him will experience this same resurrection.[10]

The new heaven and new earth will be established *here*, where God will dwell among us, just as he intended in Eden. Skye Jethani describes it as "neither an ethereal heaven nor a replaced earth. It is the union of heaven and earth into a restored and glorified cosmos occupied by God and his people."[11] There will be no more tears, no more death, no more division, no more weeping, no more suffering, no more brokenness. All will be made whole.

What glorious hope we have in that! Jennifer Dukes Lee says "hope is a midwife, helping us to breathe,"[12] and she's exactly right. We grieve now with hope because we know death (and the pain associated with it) does not have the final word. Life does.

Even now, as you consider the longing in your heart for your baby, know that your longing points to the kingdom of heaven—the realm of Jesus where all follows him in renewal. It exposes your desire for things to be set right, made whole, restored. And that desire is good. Let your longing for your baby be a signpost to reveal the way of Jesus and the kingdom of heaven, where there are no tears and where death is swallowed up once and for all. And then live like heaven is breaking through right here, right now. Because it is. It's coming through *him* in *you*.

Is there still a lot the Bible doesn't explicitly say about how or when the renewal of all things will take place? Of course! Like the apostle Paul, we must admit, "Now we see things imperfectly, like puzzling reflections in a mirror, but then we will see everything with perfect clarity. All that I know now is partial and incomplete, but then I will know everything completely, just as God now knows me completely" (1 Cor. 13:12). But although we see things imperfectly, there's enough evidence in scripture to give us confidence that this is not just wishful thinking—this is our Christian assurance, our *hope*: All things will be made new. There is more in the age to come than sitting on clouds with our harps.

God has eternity to redeem our suffering, and it will be more beautiful than we ever thought possible.

But, as it is written,

> "What no eye has seen, nor ear heard,
> nor the heart of man imagined,
> what God has prepared for those who love him." (2:9 ESV)

"I Don't *Want* Her to Be in Heaven"

A few weeks after my first miscarriage, I asked Ryan if he would listen to a couple of songs that had been ministering to my soul as I grieved. One was called "Amy's Song" by Jonathan David Helser, and the other was "I Will Carry You" by Selah. Both were about little baby girls gone too soon.

These songs helped wrap words around what I was feeling while also validating the sorrow I felt and the reality of both the suffering and hope that I carried. I would play them when I felt I needed a good cry to release all of my big, inexpressible emotions. I still play them every now and then to remember.

When the songs finished playing for Ryan, he sat in the quiet, head hung low, tears carving down his neck.

"Aren't they beautiful?" I baited, hoping for some sort of verbal response. But he just cried in silence.

"I don't want her to be in heaven," he finally responded. "I don't want Jesus to look after her. I wanted *us* to look after her."

And this is the tension in which we live: We have the hope of a life with our babies one day, but that day is not now. There will come a time when Jesus makes all things new, and we are able to enjoy life, free of suffering and heartache, the way God always intended for us. But that time is not now. And we ache to know: What exactly does this hope mean for the tiny souls we never got to hold in our arms? Will we have a chance to mother them in the age to come? Friend, I don't know the details of that. But we can cling to this: These tiny souls are held by the presence of Jesus now, and when he makes all things new, he will make *all things new*. How could this exclude our little ones?

Although I'm still learning about the resurrection and the implications for us in the age to come, we have every reason to believe that our little ones are a part of God's great renewal plan. They are not excluded from God's intent to wipe our tears, dwell with us, and give us life without the threat of death when heaven and earth are made new and he establishes his reign among us.[13]

Death Could Not Hold Him Back

There was a cemetery near our old house that I used to walk to while still in the thick of grieving Scarlett. I would weave among the headstones, wishing I had one to call our own, until one day I found ours.

A sandstone cross stretched well over my head but at its feet a crumpled Mary engulfed the base. Her robes, also carved in sandstone, connected her from the cross to the earth, and her arms wrapped around the place where her son's feet emptied of the blood she had helped create. I can't remember the name or epitaph carved into that stunning memorial, but I will never forget the sense of identification I felt with the heartbroken mother of our Lord. She hadn't just lost Jesus, the Messiah; she had lost her son. As I considered her loss in light of mine, I realized grief connected her to both heaven and earth there among the folds of her robe. I saw it with my own eyes in the statue, but I felt it in my soul.

Our humanity and his divinity are intertwined, and nothing helps us feel that connection like the thin place between life and death—the liminal space—that grief introduces us to.

The crucifixion and resurrection of Jesus remind us that beautiful things will rise out of our ashes, and we'll find an invitation that's been there all along—new possibilities, a summoning to trust and let go, opportunities pulling us into hope. There is one whose job description is to steal, kill, and destroy, but that isn't God.[14] God takes what is meant to destroy us and turns it inside out. Instead of an end, death is transformed into a beginning. A tomb into a womb. New life. Grace like Scarlett. A redemption story that makes a mockery of what the evil one hoped would be our undoing. It starts with our resurrected Jesus and continues as we live our lives in him.

It's a miracle, truly, this upside-down way of Jesus. This God making all things new. This promise we can hold on to even while the whole earth around us is still groaning for deliverance between what is and what will be. And we don't just survive this *in between*, biding our time until some arbitrary future date when all is set right. We participate in the new creation *now* by living into the kingdom, setting our eyes on things above and things around us, and allowing the Spirit to heal us as we work together to see the whole earth healed and reconciled unto Jesus. We embrace our belovedness and give ourselves to love others even while still being healed ourselves. We bake the casserole. We write the bereavement card. We open our doors. We share our stories. We tell of his goodness. We worship while we weep. We rejoice while we give thanks. We pray for healing. We invite others to know the astonishing hope we have. We participate in his new creation and live heaven right here, right now. We dive deep and then resurface, transformed and transforming.

Your kingdom come, your will be done, on earth as it is in heaven.

Death could not hold him back. And it won't hold him back from you now. We have so much hope, such good news—a Love nothing can separate us from.

Thirteen

And Then She Laughed

*I*t was late. The children slept while Ryan watched a movie and I retreated to the warmth of our bedroom.

My grief was still a few weeks fresh, and although my days were regaining a semblance of normalcy, nightfall tended to bring my sorrow along with it. Predictable like a liturgy, my grief would rise as the sun would set.

Many nights, like this one, I would curl up in bed journaling, reading, or sipping tea and listening to music that held me in its melody. Darkness can make the world feel small, and sometimes small feels safe and good. This night was like that.

Salt-heavy tears burned tracks down my cheeks as I thought of what we had lost. More than anything, I was sad. I missed our baby. I wanted her back.

Let the little children come to me, I felt Jesus whisper.[1]

At one time Jesus spoke of the little ones gathered around him for a blessing, but that night he spoke right into my spirit about Scarlett, and about all the little ones lost to the heartbroken mothers and fathers who joined me in the fellowship of suffering.

Let them come to me, he said again.

Our baby was already gone, but I knew what he meant. Would I be willing to let go? Would I release this child to Jesus, knowing she was already safe in his arms anyway? I don't believe God took our child, but I will never doubt he received her the moment her tiny heart stopped beating.

He said it to me on that lonely night, and he continues to this day: *Let the children come to me. Let them come.*

> Jesus said, "Let the little children come to me and do not hinder them, for to such belongs the kingdom of heaven." (Matt. 19:14 ESV)

Releasing my babies to Jesus does not mean denying they belong to our family. Letting go doesn't bypass my grief or "bring closure" or help me *move on.* (We don't move on from the loss of our children, as if we've changed jobs or given up a fashion trend.)

But there comes a time when we begin to *move forward.* And to move forward, we have to let go of what we don't have. We have to give these little ones to Jesus.

No one can tell you what this will look like or mean to you. No one can assign you a time frame. No one can prescribe your path forward.

My babies are not coming back. Neither are yours. And I hate that. Their lives mean something; our babies matter. Life *always* matters. Our loss is bitter and our grief is warranted. But we cannot hold on to them. At least not how we once imagined.

Making peace with our loss doesn't mean we stop aching. It doesn't mean we forget. It doesn't mean we "get over it" or that our tears will be dried up. Making peace with our loss means we trust Jesus enough to carry us and nurture us as we attend to the vulnerable, gritty, sacred work of growing through our grief into the rest of our lives. Making peace with our loss means we release our babies to the hope of heaven, knowing God will sustain us in our lack. He will teach us how to live all over again.

> I will strengthen you and help you.
> I will hold you up with my victorious right hand.
>
> (Isa. 41:10)

As I've practiced this *letting go* over the years and through my miscarriages (because letting go is *not* a one-time event), I've often thought of Jochebed, Moses's mother.[2] How did it feel to let her son go? She knew she couldn't keep him. What happened to her mother's heart as she realized she couldn't control his destiny—whether he would live or die? How did it feel to see him taken to Pharaoh's palace, knowing his every need would be attended to—the whole kingdom at his fingertips!—while also knowing he *should* have been in her home? Like Ryan, did she say "But I wanted *us* to look after him"? Did her arms feel empty? Did she grieve the future they would never have together? Did *her* life turn upside down as she was forced to let go?

You and I can know our babies are safe in the presence of Jesus, that their every need is met, that they'll want for nothing. We can be reassured they're "in a better place" (as well-meaning friends like to remind us), but it doesn't erase the pain of letting them go. Still, we must. We simply cannot hang on.

Letting go hurts and it heals; God's made provision for both.

And as we let go of what we cannot keep, we begin to realize we can't keep the old version of ourselves, either. The paradox, then, is that by loosening our grip and letting go of what can't be kept, our hands become open to receive something new.

Becoming You. Again.

Grief changes a person. You and I are not the same women we were before losing babies. Although our identity in Christ has not changed, how we give expression to our lives may have. The essence of who we are is still intact, but the way we absorb what we see around us is now filtered through eyes that have seen the underside of sorrow. Grief expands the soul and exposes our need, but it also expands our heart to receive love and be changed by it. This *becoming* can make us more whole if we are open to receive (and be changed by) God's astonishing love.

"Blessed are those who mourn," Jesus said, "for they shall be comforted" (Matt. 5:4 ESV). We are not blessed because we are mourning what was lost; we are blessed because we've experienced his comfort in the midst of it—*that's* the blessing. Suddenly the brokenness has been transformed into the blessing. He doesn't simply want to rescue us; he wants to remake us. How stunning!

"You are the light of the world," Jesus goes on to say to all the people he's just blessed (the mourners, the poor in spirit, the meek, the persecuted, and others).[3] Don't miss this, friend. Blessing for the world comes through you too. You who mourn are among those he will use to light up the whole earth. The very fact that you've received his comfort means you have something to give—your need and your bounty tied together into one. It's so upside-down! It's so amazing!

One of my favorite children's authors, Sally Lloyd-Jones, writes about those whom God uses to light the world with his light and love:

> Who would make good helpers, do you think? Clever ones? Rich ones? Strong, important ones? Some people might think so, but I'm sure by now you don't need me to tell you they'd be wrong. Because the people God uses don't have to know a lot of things, or have a lot of things—they just have to need him a lot.[4]

Are you beginning to see it yet? God can, and longs to, use you just as you are—brokenness and all.

The Gift of Vision

When I visited his farm in North Carolina for the first time, my friend Ken led me up a ridge to show me a gazebo his son Jonathan had built. Jonathan had named it the "prayerzebo," and for years it's been a place of prayer and communion and song writing. On our way back, Ken paused. "See out that direction?" He pointed. "You can see the mountains through there during the winter." That's all he said, but I *heard* more.

We often think of winter as the season when things are hard to see. Winter is when the blizzards come; it's when the fog rolls in. We shiver and shudder, staring at the calendar, willing the page to turn. But in the desolate season of barren trees you can see farther ahead, and on through, than you can when life is in full bloom. Losing someone you love can feel like winter. A blizzard might hit, sure, but when it passes and you regain your ability to see, there's a certain grace to see farther, even in the middle of all that emptiness.

There will come a time when you realize the blizzard is over. The fog has lifted. The questions you must ask yourself then are: *What can I see now through the trees? What does the winter want to teach me? Can I discern farther?*

Grief can be a wonderful clarifier. In the aftermath of losing Oliver, it was as if God drew things into sharp focus for Ryan and me. Our life felt short, and we wanted our days to count. Unimportant things melted away. The voices (real or imagined) of those who might discourage us from pursuing different dreams seemed to hold less power. The fears that had potential to hold us back came under the scrutiny of our desire to live our one precious life well, *and this was good*. We made some of the best decisions of our lives during this time. This post-blizzard winter clarity was a gift.

And Then Comes Spring

I can't tell you how long your winter will last, but I can tell you it won't be forever. The liminal space of grief isn't infinite. When the ground is frozen over and the trees seem at a standstill, there's much work going on under the surface. Those roots are digging deep to find the nourishment they need. And when they do—when the roots have gone deep enough to have found their source—they will provide the grid for growth come springtime.

You'll be amazed at how the buds and branches and leaves push through when the sun reappears, cradling the earth in her warmth and calling new life to come. You'll begin to recognize the transformation, which was hard to see from the inside, and you'll marvel at how God worked a miracle while you were barely looking.

All things new. This continues to be his redemption story—the resurrection, the reconciliation of all things. Light bursting through the darkness. It's the kingdom of God at hand—always new, always coming alive, always growing into something that looks like Jesus.

It's such good news—the kind of good news that allows us to have hope while still in the middle of grieving.

What Can I Give from the Middle?

Sometimes the most beautiful stories are the ones told from the middle, the ones without happy endings. It can be romantic to see a rescuer save the distressed in order to live happily ever after, but what if that's not enough? What if, in addition to the happily ever afters, we *also* need to hear and see demonstrations of God's faithfulness in our lives right from the middle of our stories— stories of resilience from within hardship, stories of hope while we're still in the dark?

In Hebrews 11, we see story after story of those we would consider "heroes of faith" who never saw their happy endings come to fruition or God's promises fulfilled. Consider Sarah (Sarai), the jealous woman who drove Hagar out of their home when contempt over Hagar's pregnancy thrust the relationship into chaos. (We looked at their story in chapter 4.) Thousands of years later, you and I have seen Sarah's unfolding story as her people (the nation of Israel) multiplied to fill the earth. But could Sarah see the *nation* that would come from her ninety-year-old barren womb when she stood there in the middle? Could she see how the whole earth would be blessed?

What about you, friend? Are you still in the "middle chapters" now? You may think you have nothing to offer until the chaos is resolved: *I don't yet know my redemption story.* Or you might size up your experiences and determine they're pretty unremarkable: *How could my life make a difference in someone else's?*

Whatever your assessment of your story, you won't know how it can help and heal others until you pour it out. I'm not just talking about the literal story of your miscarriage here; I'm talking about your life. Your messy, ordinary, extraordinary, beautiful life.

I was so tempted to put off writing this book until I was sure I could package it all up with a happy ending and wouldn't have to write *to* the trenches *from* the trenches, but I continued to sense God's nudge to link arms and do this with you, not as your leader but as your companion. Two days after saying *yes* to God's prompting to begin writing this book (while I was in Tuscany), I had my second miscarriage, and then a year later I had my third. These stories and words have been like mining gold from the rubble through two miscarriages, an arduous pregnancy that left me unable to walk for months, and the hazy, sleepless (wonderful) newborn days of our sixth child. The truth is, I'm still on this grief journey too. I've been healed and I'm still healing. Even this book is a miracle—a testament to God's faithfulness while we're still in the middle.

But what if my story can't heal anyone? And what if yours can't either?

The enemy of our souls works tirelessly to sow doubt and insecurity into our minds. But here's the good news: Our stories can't heal others, but Jesus can *and does* as we offer them.

Transformation and healing are his work, not ours, but he uses surrendered lives and authentic stories as a vehicle to communicate his revolutionary love. He's done it since the beginning of time, and he'll keep on doing it until the whole of our collective volumes looks like *his* redemption story.

I love Eugene Peterson's interpretation of Jesus's words and intent as he addresses the crowds during the Sermon on the Mount: "Keep open house; be generous with your lives. By opening up to others, you'll prompt people to open up with God, this generous Father in heaven" (Matt. 5:16 MSG).

This has proven true over and over again in my own life: The more I'm willing to give voice to the work of God within me, the more others open up and give voice to the work of God in their lives. Story begets story. Vulnerability begets vulnerability. Declarations of hope beget hope. Offerings of love beget love. And as that happens, our stories—bathed in the sacrifice of Jesus—do the actual work of overcoming the darkness.[5] This is amazing, powerful, ordinary-sacred stuff.

Our Stories Change the World

A friend once asked me if it's helped to share my stories so frankly with friends, family, and readers who are often complete strangers. She wondered if it's hard to open myself up, knowing it gives invitation for others to share about their own heartache and pain and knowing they might need comforting too.

And here's my answer to her question: I believe part of the way we heal is by helping to heal others. When I am open about my pain, I invite God (and others) into those hard spaces to look at pain too—my own, but also *theirs*. When I am free with my life and faith in the way I give myself to others, I also free myself to receive. You have to release your grip to give, but you also have to release it to receive. Open hands are hands that can't hoard love and truth and comfort; they are positioned to both give and receive. And openness of heart and hands requires vulnerability—this, I strongly believe.

Have you chosen to open your life to others around you who are hurting? Have you asked God to open your eyes to see those you may have overlooked before you knew grief?

From the middle, we have the power to choose our response. Jerry Sittser puts it this way:

> Choice is therefore the key. We can run from the darkness, or we can enter into it and face the pain of loss. We can indulge ourselves in self-pity, or we can empathize with others and embrace their pain as our own. We can run away from sorrow and drown it in addictions, or we can learn to live with sorrow. We can nurse wounds of having been cheated in life, or we can be grateful and joyful, even though there seems to be little reason for it. We can return evil for evil, or we can overcome evil with good. It is this power to choose that adds dignity to our humanity and gives us the ability to transcend our circumstances, thus releasing us from living as mere victims.[6]

What if we're stronger than we think?

What if the middle is a gift too?

What if how we go from here can give meaning to our grief?

What if we lived our own redemption story right here, right now, calling "Kingdom, come!" even while our hearts are still broken? What if we found joy intermixed with our grief?

What if we became known not just by our shared pain but by our shared hope?

What if we lived our lives as they are, not as they were? And what if we dared to live into them as they will be one day—on earth as it is in heaven?

> She is clothed with strength and dignity,
>   and she laughs without fear of the future. (Prov. 31:25)

Part VI
Invitation

Journal Prompt: Write a letter to your baby, telling her all the things you wish she knew about you, your family, and the dreams you had for your future. Choose one or two of these prompts to write about: Tell him how you feel about him. Tell her how (or if) your dreams are changing now that she is gone. Will you give yourself permission to dream again? If so, tell him about it. How do you hope your grief and suffering can be transformed into a gift? How is this loss changing you already? How do you feel about your future?

Acknowledgments

Since this is my first book, I feel like I have a lifetime of people to thank. But first, Jesus: Only you know the extent of what this book cost us, so to you I want to say from the depths of my being: You are worth it, and so much more. May this offering be sweet. Thank you for carrying and sustaining and teaching me, for comforting and encouraging me, for inspiring me, discipling me, and loving me at my darkest. My whole life has been changed by your goodness. I love you.

To Jenni Burke, my agent and friend: It's impossible to imagine this book's existence without your steady presence in my life. You saw something in me that I sometimes *still* have to squint to see. Thank you for your wisdom, expertise, and affirmation; your investment in my life and career; and—most of all—your beautiful, faithful friendship. *Ti amo la sorella di mia anima.*

To my publishing team at Baker Books: I'm so glad you saw the urgency for meeting this need. Thank you for taking a chance on me and for being a midwife to this message. I'm especially grateful to Rebekah Guzman for immediately grasping the vision for this project and for believing in me as an author when I was still getting used to the idea myself. I'm so grateful! To Patti

Brinks for your intuition, inclusiveness, and creative direction, and to Mayuko Fujino for your spectacular art. Collaborating with the two of you to design this cover was one of the greatest joys of this project. To Nicci Jordan Hubert, your editorial input and affirmation have meant more to me than you'll ever know. Thank you for putting wind in my sails when I needed it. Your first email to me after reading my manuscript might be pinned on my bulletin board forever and ever, amen. To Lindsey Spoolstra and the entire editorial team for seeing this through to completion—thank you.

To my Book Doula Girls for helping pray this book into existence and to the Booker Family Prayer Team, especially Sue, Sandi, Alicia, Marsha, Jess, Eleanor, Grandma Ola, and Grandma Mac: You—along with all the others who pray for us—are God's generous gift to our family.

To Becca de Souza, Mia Giltinan, Erika Morrison, Alia Hagenbach, Bethany Bassett, Jessica Wolstenholm, Amber Haines, Jennifer Dukes Lee, Lisa Jacobsen, Tsh Oxenreider, and Maria Furlough: For every tear I've cried while writing this book, your encouragement surpasses it tenfold. You've kept me company over Voxer and held my hand as I poured my guts into the keyboard and became an author. Thank you. And to Amber in particular: I barely know how to thank you for your breathtaking foreword. It means the world to me—you mean the world to me. Thank you.

To Jim Stephens, Ken Helser, Bo Stern, Nancie Carmichael, Mrs. Hurley, Myquillan Smith, and Emily Freeman: Thank you for mentoring me, even when you didn't realize you were. I love the way you offer your words and hearts to the world. To my Hope*Writers friends, especially my Shop Talk girls, Grief Circle girls, Brian, and Gary: Your feedback, solidarity, and cheerleading throughout my creative process (and my angst!) have been invaluable.

To Dania Watson, Tiffany Lausen, Jason Deutscher, and Ryan Cheney: Thank you for your creative talent and professional expertise, your investment of time, and for recognizing this as an extension of our family's ministry. To our YWAM supporters: This book is yours too. Thank you for believing in us and standing by us when we needed you.

To our YWAM Australia family, whom we cherish: Thank you for befriending me, mentoring me, growing with me, and having so much fun these last seventeen years. You'll always be my tribe. This, too, is part of our wave.

To Sister Maximilian for mothering me when I needed it most. To my Tuscany Writers' Retreat comrades: Thank you for meeting me under the stairs and showing me Jesus among the olive groves. Gelato culture always, hallelujah. To the many precious people who supported us in our grief—too many to name: Thank you for showing up. You are beautiful.

To Mia and Dave, Misti and Randy: You and your littles are our people. My heart aches with gratitude for the gift you've been to our family. Love you fiercely, Happy People. To Pastors Steve and Suzanne, Pastors Ken and Linda, and Pastors Glenn and Gabby for continuing to believe in us throughout the many changes and growing pains in all of our lives and ministries. To Emma, Patrina, Sarah, Kris, Tania, JP, Slone, and Mel—your friendship is a gift.

To The Lovelies, the Love A Mama Collective, and my amazing community of readers: Thank you for your years of faithfulness. I want to hug each of you. Like, *for reals.* To the storytellers at Our Scarlett Stories and the countless women and men who have shared heartbreak and hope with me: Thank you for trusting me with your stories. May you meet with God again in these pages.

To my parents, Gwen and Scott, and my in-laws, Bob and Sylvia: You have given me the greatest gifts in life. How can I express my gratitude? I love you and Andy, Ben and Koz, and our whole wonderful family. You have my heart.

To Levi, Judah, and Micah: I never thought having sons could make a mama so proud. You've set my heart ablaze, and I'm so thankful to share life with you. I adore you. Thank you for all the ways you helped me write this book, and for ensuring my cup always runneth over. Together let's always be brave, be kind, be curious, and know that we are loved, okay?

To Ryan, the love of my life: Thank you for all of the flat whites and flowers and green curries you set next to my keyboard without prompting. Thank you for talking me off the ledge one million times and for your relentless belief in me. The way you have loved me, served me, and championed me during our first decade of marriage is stunning—I see Jesus all over, and in, and through you. You have my gratitude, my admiration, and my deepest love.

To our little ones, Scarlett, Ollie, and Ruby: You are cherished. Our time together is coming.

Appendix A

A Letter for Grieving Dads

*D*ear Fellow Dad,

I'm deeply sorry for your loss. A man should never have to say *goodbye* to his child before *hello*. I don't know how you're coping, but if you're anything like me, you feel like a walking paradox of mixed emotions and questions. Not only are you dealing with the loss of your baby but you're also seeing your wife in pain and wondering how to best comfort her, while also trying to work out your own response to a loss that feels so abstract. My hope is that openly sharing my experiences will spur you to process your own complicated emotions in a way that makes sense to you and brings life to your marriage and family.

First, I want to give you permission to acknowledge this as a terrible loss. Growing up in Australia, I didn't feel this permission was modeled to me—it certainly wasn't the default among men. I wonder if you can relate. The expectation here has been that men are tough, provide for the physical needs of their family, and remain strong at all costs. Thankfully some of the outdated "macho" attitudes and gender roles are changing as we parent the younger generation, but these norms are still deeply ingrained in our culture. We've got to work our way out of them even as we try to change them.

Lost for Words

I was thirty-nine years old when we experienced our first miscarriage, and I had no idea how to deal with it. I can't recall ever hearing much about pregnancy loss before we experienced ours, and can't remember a single conversation I had with another man about this kind of grief. We discuss other important issues at the pub with our mates, at church, on social media, on the news, and at work, but miscarriage still feels taboo among men, like somehow it's a secret women's problem that we simply need to help them "deal" with as quietly as possible so that no one gets embarrassed or uncomfortable. It's easy to get the impression that a loss like this is inconsequential and small.

After our first miscarriage, I wanted to talk openly about it but felt lost for words. There was a disconnect between the way I felt I *should* feel and the way I *actually* felt. No one needed to convince me that something weighty had happened in our family, but I had no cultural framework to know how to begin the conversation. In retrospect, I think I tried to help myself by helping my wife—if she felt better, then I would feel better too.

With each miscarriage, I clicked into survival mode—caring for Adriel and our other children, organizing meals, answering phone calls, and so on, as if I didn't have time to be emotional over it. Maybe there was a certain grace to enable me for that role in the early days, and I think that response is appropriate. But the problem comes when we never revisit those emotions. If we stuff them down or turn them off in order to be the "strong one," they have a way of eating at us from the inside. Unresolved grief can create a roadblock between you and your wife or you and God at a time when you need those relationships most.

My Wife and I Grieved Differently

Another barrier for me was that I found it hard to even wrap my head around the loss in the beginning. Although I was so excited to be having a baby, it was all still so conceptual. I watched my wife grieve in a way that was foreign to me. I'd never seen her in such pain. From the moment she knew she was pregnant, she felt intimately connected to the baby. It's incredible how quickly hormones kick in and start to change a woman's body during pregnancy. A baby affects her entire existence. I've always thought that sort of connection from the "inside" creates a bond that's hard for fathers to relate to until the baby is actually in our arms. (At least that's been my experience.)

I had to wrestle down my own *shoulds* during that time: I should be more sad, I should grieve more like Adriel, I should know how to talk about this, and so on. I had to learn to accept that miscarriage affected us differently and that this was okay, even normal. I needed to be secure in my own process and let my grief take its own shape.

As an individual, you, too, will process grief in your own way, and it might look very different from your wife's grief journey (or mine). I hope you have the courage to give yourself permission to lean in to the process and let the grief work its way through your soul so you can heal and grow. You might be surprised at the grace God releases for you to not only deal with your pain but experience him more deeply in the midst of it.

Finally, I want to offer a few practical suggestions in hopes these might serve you.

1. Find a Way to Give Identity to Your Baby

We did this by naming each one. It may seem like a small thing, but it wasn't. Giving them names with thoughtful meanings helped me think of them as real members of our family. I know some couples feel uncomfortable choosing a name when the baby is still so tiny or when you may not know the gender. If so, consider choosing a gender-neutral name or even a nickname. Whether you decide to keep the name private or share it with others, giving your child a name will help your loss feel more palpable, which can be helpful in the grieving process.

2. Consider How to Commemorate Your Baby's Life and Say Goodbye

Along with our kids, Adriel and I did a simple goodbye ceremony by writing messages on helium balloons for each of our babies in the weeks after the miscarriages. I was surprised at how good and healing it felt to do something together that would build an experiential memory. Holding the balloons in my hand before seeing them float into the sky created an image in my mind that I'll always treasure. Take some time together with your wife and find something that suits your family culture. (For more ideas, see appendix B.)

3. Let Your Wife See Your Grief

You might be tempted to think you need to keep it together in order to help your wife "get over" her grief, but from what I've seen in my own marriage (and among friends, as we've learned to talk about this more openly), is that most women want and need to know you're grieving too. She doesn't want to be *fixed*, she wants to be *together*. When she sees this matters to you, she'll draw comfort from knowing she doesn't have to grieve alone. Processing grief together can also help you get in touch with your own emotions if you're finding it challenging.

4. Pull Toward Your Wife, Not Away

Weather the storm together, and ask God to build intimacy and resiliency in your marriage as you support each other in your grief.

Experiencing heartache together can strengthen or weaken a marriage, so be intentional to turn toward each other instead of away.

5. Be Intentional to Remember

Mark important dates on your calendar—such as the date of the miscarriage and the baby's original due date—and be sensitive around other special days like Mother's Day and Christmas. Do something small but intentional to let your wife know you haven't forgotten. Tell her you miss your baby too.

I don't think our culture has done us any favors by shielding us from the reality of miscarriage and other types of pregnancy loss, or imposing the notion on us that men have to be the "strong" or silent ones while our wives grieve. Maybe, as we take steps of humility and transparency with our wives and with each other, we can change the conversation and grow more whole together. Perhaps you and I are the ones to help break the stigma surrounding pregnancy loss so future bereaved fathers will feel less isolated and more supported as they grieve—imagine the freedom and healing that would follow.

May you sense God's nearness in your time of loss.

Warmly,

Ryan Booker (Adriel's husband)

Appendix B
Remembering Your Baby (Memorial Ideas)

Many parents find it helpful in their grieving process to do something deliberate to honor their baby. Some choose to commemorate their baby at the time of miscarriage (or soon after) while others choose to honor their baby in ongoing ways through yearly rituals. Still others choose not to do anything formal at all. There is no right or wrong to this—do what feels right to you personally.

Here are a few ideas:

1. Name your baby.
2. Choose a symbol that represents your baby, so that every time you see it, you'll have a sweet reminder of them (such as a sparrow, butterfly, or rose).
3. Buy or make a piece of jewelry that includes your baby's birthstone or is engraved with your baby's birthday or name.

4. Release butterflies, floating lanterns, or balloons with messages of remembrance or goodbye attached.

5. Plant a tree or flowers. Consider finding something that will likely bloom at a special time each year (such as the baby's birthday or Mother's Day).

6. Invite your family or small circle of friends for a memorial service at a place that has significance for you.

7. Commemorate your baby with a garden stone or small garden statue that has meaning to you. (Bury the remains of your baby, if you are able to.)

8. Buy a windchime that will remind you of your baby every time you hear the wind blow through.

9. Get a tattoo with a symbol that holds special meaning. (Popular ideas include your baby's name, due date, a special flower such as forget-me-nots, or butterflies.)

10. Frame an ultrasound photo or a photo of your baby bump to display with other family photos.

11. Participate in a walk of remembrance in honor of your baby.

12. Donate in your baby's name to the March of Dimes, SIDS research, a children's hospital, the Ronald McDonald House, the World Health Organization, the Love A Mama Collective, Every Mother Counts, a pregnancy loss support group such as Hope Mommies, or another organization or charity.

13. Create something: Compose a song, write a poem, create artwork, write a prayer, share a blog post or social media tribute, knit a blanket, or embroider a keepsake.

14. Make a memory box to store ultrasound photos, sympathy cards, a hospital band, or any other small items that hold special meaning.

15. Buy a Christmas ornament representing your child that you can bring out each year and add to your family Christmas tree.

16. Choose a date to commemorate each year and do something special to remember your baby, either privately or with your family or friends.
17. Write a letter to your baby each year on their birthday, perhaps in a journal.
18. Light a candle and take some personal time to reflect on other "marker" dates such as your due date, Pregnancy Loss Awareness Day (October 15), Mother's Day, Father's Day, and so forth.

For more ideas, please visit www.AdrielBooker.com/miscarriage -memorial-ideas.

Helping Your Child Process Grief after Miscarriage

I cried when Ryan brought lunch to me in our home office and informed me Fishy Coco was dead.

It wasn't that I was particularly fond of the fish. Fish don't have much personality, and I understand their fleeting life span and how humans can easily ruin them if we're not careful. I knew the fragility of life in the fishbowl when I bought him, but the measured risk felt worth it in order to do something special during a difficult time.

I never imagined a little fighting fish could be a symbol of hope and new life while I grieved, but that's exactly what he was when I took the hand of three-year-old Levi and made a big deal about choosing our first family pet together in aisle six of the Pet Emporium.

For months I checked that stupid fish multiple times a day for signs of life. I realize how silly it sounds, but somehow that fish was wrapped up in my expectations of life sustained, and conquering hard stuff, and the balance of things being right in the world. I just needed him to keep living. That very morning I had ensured he was still alive—my little piece of life safely contained in a pretty glass bowl. As I verified his still-rippling fins, I muttered curse words under my breath at the insanity of getting him in the first place when I was terrified he would die and force me to hold my son's face in my hands and explain death to him again.

I was secretly afraid that a dead fish would break him. (Or break me.)

But instead, Levi marched up to me and announced: "Fishy Coco is dead, Mama. Daddy 'fushed' him down the toilet." And that was that.

Levi never blamed anyone or asked *why* or even got upset. Things live and die; apparently he embraced this reality just as concretely as he knew dinner would appear on the table sometime around 6:00 p.m.

I never expected my small child to have the capacity to let go so easily. But this was our life after loss.

Obviously, losing a fish is completely different than losing a baby or a relative or a friend (or even a beloved family dog or cat), but the ease with which he accepted death still surprised me.

His indifference toward losing Fishy Coco also assured me he was cognizant of the difference between a fighting fish and the baby he never saw. For months, out of the blue he would say things like, "I miss the baby, Mama. I feel sad." Or, "I wish the baby coulda' come home instead of go'd to heaven." He never said such things about the fish.

Knowing about our miscarriage also instilled a new depth of empathy in our young son. Now and then he would notice I was a bit misty-eyed or quiet and would say, "Are you sad about the baby today, Mama?" If I responded with a *yes*, he would say, "Me too," and give me a hug or crawl into my lap for a cuddle. My initial worry about burdening him was replaced with the joy of seeing him operate as a little healer—beginning to realize his own capacity to care for others in their pain. Perhaps he was more sad about seeing me sad than he was about losing the baby, but either way the response that followed was precious.

Because we were open about our loss and our heartache, Levi was actively learning to be open about the stirrings of his own heart and soul too. (And this was repeated and deepened after our next two miscarriages, as both Levi and Judah got older and continued to comprehend more.)

Though I'm not thankful our miscarriages happened, I'll always appreciate the experience of grieving together as a family in our kids' early days, and I'll always believe these events played a part in building the empathy we so easily recognize in their lives today.

Being a child's first teacher is one of the greatest honors of parenthood, and there's no better environment to tackle the vulnerabilities and challenges of life together than within the safety of our nurturing love. Home is a learning ground for all of life, and although we can't teach our kids how to respond to every possible situation they may encounter later in life, we can do our best to teach them principles and values about how to respond to the important ones. Further, as people of faith, these issues of life and death are central to our belief system, so why would we shelter our kids from learning about something so important?

I realize that while you're grieving you may not be thinking extensively about this opportunity to help nurture your child's heart. The desire may be there, but the capacity to think it through may not be. The following are some practical suggestions for how to help your kids process their grief, should you choose to include them. (I respect that some parents feel it's best not to, and that others cannot include their children for varied reasons. As a parent, you're the one most suited to determine what's best for your family.) This list is not intended to be exhaustive, and I encourage you to access resources from professionals who specialize in dealing with childhood grief as needed.

1. Be honest with your kids.

Kids intuit so much that even if you tried to hide your grief from them, chances are they'd still suspect something is going on. Being honest with them about what happened not only gives them understanding as to what they're picking up from your behavior or the undercurrent in your home but also gives them a chance to learn how to process heartache within the safest environment they know—your family.

2. Avoid euphemisms.

Use simple and accurate words to describe what happened. If you say, "Mommy lost the baby," your young child might misinterpret your words and become fearful of you losing her too. Don't say things like "The baby is sleeping," or "The baby is an angel now." Because these are untrue, they can be confusing for a young child to process (i.e., they might think, *If I go to sleep will I, too, never wake up?*). Instead, be honest while still using age-appropriate language. For a younger child this might be: "The baby in Mommy's tummy died." For an older child you might say: "We found out the baby's heart stopped beating. This means the baby has not only stopped growing but has died. The doctors aren't sure why it happened." The Child Mind Institute suggests starting with the minimum amount of (accurate) information and then adding more based on the questions they ask.[1]

3. Welcome their questions.

Some children are naturally more inquisitive than others, but all children are curious, whether they know how to verbalize their curiosity or not. Encourage question-asking by inviting their questions. For example, you could ask, "Is there anything you'd like to know about Mommy's visit to the hospital after the baby died?" or "If you could ask Jesus one thing about our baby, what would you ask?" You could also ask open-ended questions to get conversation started, such as "How did you feel when we told you the baby has died?" or "How do you feel when you see that Mommy is sad?"

4. Be willing to say, "I don't know."

If you have answers to your child's questions, then answer them honestly. But if not, don't pretend you do or sidestep the question. It's tempting to be fearful that admitting we don't know will undermine our child's confidence at a time they need it most, but admitting we don't know the answers can be a powerful tool of identification and connection. Your humility can instill confidence in them as they see you trust them enough to be vulnerable. If answers are available, commit to looking for them together (such as searching scripture to learn more about heaven).

5. Alleviate their emotional stress.

As you help your child process, preemptively address some common concerns, even if they haven't been able to articulate them. Make sure they understand it's not their fault. (Perhaps they secretly felt jealous of the baby and now worry they somehow contributed to the miscarriage.) Tell them that although you're upset about the baby dying, you're not upset with them.

6. Process through reading, writing, art, and play.

Read age-appropriate storybooks on loss and grief (see appendix F). Encourage them to draw a picture that describes what happened or how they feel now. Play a few different songs and ask them to choose one that sounds like how they feel. If your child is older, encourage them to write how they feel perhaps through a series of back-and-forth journaling with you, or give them a prompt to write their response to, such as writing a letter to Jesus about how they feel or penning a note to the baby telling her anything they'd like her to know. Give your child the space to work out their feelings toward death through normal imaginative play.

7. Receive your child's empathy and care.

Understanding that our children are human too, it's important we give them opportunity to express themselves as not just the recipients of comfort but also its givers. Open your heart to receive the care they offer. Allowing your kids the chance to minister to your soul builds something special in them as they realize that they, too, have something beautiful to offer the world. They will bless you with their kindness! And you will bless them with your humility to receive it.

8. Understand that each child will grieve differently.

Just as we respond differently to grief (we explored this in part III), children are unique individuals too. Their personality, experiences, age, and mental and emotional capacity will factor into their response. They might display behavioral problems, regression, moodiness, nightmares, magical play, fascination with death, bed-wetting, or any number of things.[2] (See appendix F for professional resources regarding grief during different developmental stages of childhood.)

9. Provide security through your environment.

As much as possible, try to maintain your family's most important routines. This might mean your weekly rhythm of game night or your one-on-one prayers before bedtime. Grief and loss *do* interrupt our lives and routines, but consider a few key areas where you can remain consistent. Having something predictable and steady will be a calming anchor in your child's day and week.

10. Make room for one-on-one time.

As you grieve, you might need some space to be alone, and I hope by this point in the book you've given yourself permission for that. Consider also that your child might need extra attention from you, and think of opportunities to meet their needs in ways you'll both find life-giving. Get down on the floor with them to play LEGOs or dress dollies, take them on a date to play UNO over milkshakes, let them spend the night in bed with you one night, ask them if they'll go on a hike with you to a favorite lookout, invite them to a café to read aloud a chapter book over hot chocolate. (If you're aware of your child's "love language," consider how you can demonstrate your love to them in ways that best fill their tank.[3])

11. Introduce or reinforce relevant aspects of your faith.

As a Christian, there's no better time to discuss your core beliefs about the afterlife. Don't embellish what we don't know, but do emphasize the promises of Jesus that there will be a time when he wipes away every tear and we will feel pain no more. Assure them your baby is safe with Jesus, and let them explore what they believe through prayer, Bible reading, and thoughtful discussion with you. Encourage them to use the gift of imagination when wondering together what heaven—life with Jesus—might be like (i.e., "I imagine heaven might . . .").

12. Use ritual or ceremony to mark your baby's life.

Create a memory that your child can look back on to mark the baby's life. Consider asking them if there's a way they'd like to remember the baby or suggest a way yourself (see appendix B for ideas).

13. Give the child a special gift or comfort item.

(This is particularly helpful for a child who seems to need extra comfort or care.) A friend of mine turned her husband's favorite shirts into "Daddy pillows" for her children to cuddle after he died.[4] You could do something similar with a special baby outfit or blanket, or you could allow the child to choose a new stuffed toy to hug and cuddle when they are missing the baby.

14. Inform care providers.

If your child goes to school or daycare, make sure their care providers and teachers know what's happened in case your child needs extra support.

15. Get professional help.

You are the best student of your child, and they will teach you what they need. If you believe they need more help processing their grief than you are equipped to give, find a qualified professional counselor who is trained in grief counseling for children.

Appendix D

Pregnancy after Loss

For many women, part of their healing is delving straight back into trying to get pregnant again. For me, that wasn't the case. After all three of my miscarriages, I needed time before I felt ready to dip my toe back into the possibility of risk.

I've now experienced three pregnancies after miscarriage, all of which were simultaneously thrilling and frightening. The gift of pregnancy is a joy, but there are no guarantees your heart will remain unscathed.

Years ago, while on a work trip to Cambodia, I toured an area that had been fraught with hidden land mines from decades of civil war, which culminated in genocide under the Khmer Rouge in the 1970s. Today these areas are known as the killing fields. While the term *killing fields* sunk in, I stood at the edge of one and tried to imagine what it would be like to know that any misstep could trigger a blast that would obliterate a body part, leave me blind, or end my life. The scope of terror and uncertainty and gruesome destruction made me sick to my stomach.

On a personal scale, pregnancy after loss can feel like stepping into a minefield. You can't know how you'll cope with the unknowns until you're there for yourself, staring down all of the possibilities while knowing you have zero control over the outcome. The uncertainty can be debilitating.

For some women, pregnancy after loss brings a watershed of relief, redemption, and hopeful anticipation. For many it brings the weight of anxiety, fear, and confusion. Likely it brings a spectrum of emotions, including all of the above and more.

Listen to These Experiences of Pregnancy after Miscarriage

I miscarried my first baby and wondered if I'd ever hold one in my arms. "Am I a mother now or not?" I questioned. I couldn't move forward fast enough. I was desperate to know I was a "real" mother. As soon as I got far enough along in my next pregnancy to feel the baby kick, I was so relieved. But until then it felt like I was walking along the edge of a cliff and could fall off any time.
—Katie

My miscarriage came after years of infertility and finally trying IVF. Our drained savings account mirrored my drained heart. I was tired and defeated. But now that I've been pregnant once, I can dare to hope it might happen again. I'm terrified but also preoccupied with thoughts of trying again—the whole thing has me feeling heartsick with longing and fear.—Erika

I already had two kids before I started having miscarriages. I started to wonder if my body had timed out and my childbearing years had come to an abrupt halt. But then I got pregnant and it "stuck." My baby is almost three years old now, but the anxiety I felt while pregnant with him was so difficult, to the point of having panic attacks. I don't know how I would have coped without seeing a professional counselor.—Gloriana

I obsessed over the question of when to start trying again. My husband was ready immediately, but I was petrified. When we started trying for another baby, I definitely didn't feel ready. I cried every time we had sex but also felt it was unfair to my husband to keep waiting. To this day I'm not sure who was right.—Jaclyn

When I first got pregnant after my miscarriage, I would tell God, "If you love me, you know I can't take any more heartbreak and will keep this baby safe." Every time I went to the bathroom I checked for blood. I was miserable, constantly wondering if God loved me enough to keep the baby alive. When I realized this one-sided bargaining was negatively affecting my faith, I was able to surrender to the process and trust him. I decided that even if something bad *did* happen, it had nothing to do with God's love for me. My fear and anxiety didn't magically disappear, but from that point on I was able to cope much easier.—Rebecca

My husband and I decided straightaway to begin trying again, but I was wracked with fear. Every month I was afraid of being disappointed by a negative pregnancy test, while also being scared it would be positive and I'd experience another miscarriage. The fear was palpable.—Lysa

When I got pregnant after my miscarriage, my grief surprised me. I thought the pregnancy would be part of my healing, and, although it was, I struggled with a ton of guilt. I felt like being happy about my new baby was betraying the one I lost, and I got sad all over again.—Amy

My miscarriage was the saddest thing that's ever happened to me. We haven't been able to have another baby yet, but hope to one day. Every month when I get my period I experience the grief of my miscarriage all over again, combined with the disappointment of not being pregnant. I never struggled with body image issues and self-loathing before, but I do now. No one told me becoming a mother would be this hard.—Lydia

I really believed my miscarriage was a freak thing. I was sad for sure, but still really hopeful we'd have a baby. When I got pregnant again I enjoyed every little bit of the pregnancy. Although I had moments of fear off and on for the first few weeks, I felt like my miscarriage gave me perspective and helped me to not take my new pregnancy for granted. I know a lot of women deal with fear and anxiety all the way through while pregnant after miscarriage, but that just wasn't my experience. I was thankful and filled with faith.—Beth

I had postpartum depression after my miscarriage and into my next pregnancy. Seeing a counselor helped me tremendously, and by the time my daughter was born I felt strong. As soon as I held her in my arms, I had such joy and relief, but a few days later a huge wave of grief hit me out of nowhere. By that time I understood this was more than the normal "baby blues," so I was quick to access the help I needed, but wow, pregnancy and birth after miscarriage were so hard.—Jessica

My first pregnancy was a surprise, but my miscarriage showed me how ready I was to have a baby. We started trying again as soon as the doctor said it was okay. Even though I had some fears, I felt determined. My determination is what helped me most to enjoy that pregnancy.—Melissa

A Daily Choice to Hope

Friend, I don't know your background or the heartache you bring to your pregnancy journey, but I suspect you're likely to have lost the simplicity of pregnancy you once enjoyed. Your innocence surrounding pregnancy may be withered, but your peace doesn't have to be. You may still be grieving, but you can also experience joy. You may be acquainted with the reality of loss, but you can still have hope. It's a myth to think that innocence and peace are one and the same, that grief and joy can't coexist, or that loss and hope are mutually exclusive.

As I write this section of the book, I'm pregnant after my third miscarriage. I didn't experience prolonged fear or anxiety while pregnant after my first miscarriage—probably because I genuinely thought it was a terrible, one-off tragedy. My level of anxiety increased during the pregnancy after my second miscarriage. And now, three miscarriages later, a firm pattern of loss has resulted in a level of fear and anxiety that's completely foreign to me. It's been almost impossible to think of my body as anything but broken. The fact that I'm still pregnant truly feels like the miracle it is.

The tension is beginning to dissipate now as I enter my third trimester, but I still have to reckon with unwelcome thoughts regularly. What if I have another miscarriage and the experience completely undoes me? What if there was enough grace for me to endure three losses but I wouldn't be able to survive a fourth? (You can see how flawed this thinking is, but it's unfair of me to ask you to hold on to hope if I'm unwilling to also acknowledge it doesn't always come easily.)

Even as multiple ultrasounds, thumping dopplers, and kicks from the inside have helped reassure me the baby is thriving, I still struggle. Every single day I have to choose to put my hope in Jesus, even while knowing my hope won't be the thing that produces a healthy baby in my arms at the end of this. It all feels so dicey.

Love Is Risky but Worth It

Losing babies has caused me to accept that there's no magic "safe" zone you enter at the twelve-week mark. When you've lived through or heard stories of a baby's heart suddenly stopping or a baby born still, an infant dying of SIDS or a child's life claimed by a tragic accident, a friend's adult son taking his life or a beloved tween dying of cancer, then you know you are never really "safe" from death no matter what age your child reaches. You know you're never truly safe from a broken heart.

Love is so risky. A mother's heart is easily broken. (And a father's is too.)

I wish I could tell you that I always view my vulnerability as a gift or that my dependence on God always feels like a blessing instead of desperation, but it wouldn't be true. I have struggled in my fragility and my inability to control outcomes. Over and over, I've needed to dive deep.

You can know all the right stuff—that the odds are in your favor, that your pregnancy is progressing normally, that there's no reason to believe a miscarriage will happen again. But when you've experienced death in your womb, you are changed from the inside and you've got to gulp hard and learn how to be the best new version of yourself.

Yes, it's hard. *But we can do hard things.*

I'm sorry if miscarriage has robbed you of the easygoing nature of pregnancy you once knew. I'm sorry if this feels scary. I'm sorry if you feel small. I'm sorry if important people in your life view your current pregnancy as a replacement for the baby you lost. I'm sorry if you're afraid of your own body. I'm sorry if you're struggling to trust God. I'm sorry if this feels impossible.

My friend John says, "Love always finds its destination," and I'm convinced he's right. I pray Love will find its way to you through the arms of a child. But if it doesn't come in that form, know this: Love can and will find you. Yes, even when your body feels broken. Maybe especially then.

Invite Jesus to Lead You

I once started to read a book about pregnancy after loss but couldn't get past the first few chapters without my blood boiling. The author told her story of how she meditated on positive thoughts and prayed positive prayers through her next pregnancy and the baby "stuck." While her story resulted in a healthy, full-term baby—which is absolutely wonderful!—it also inadvertently sent the message that pregnancies that don't make it to full term must be the fault of the mother. Perhaps she didn't think positively enough or pray enough. The book made me so angry as I thought about my in-box full of notes from hurting women; the last thing they needed was to be made to feel like they were at fault. I'm quite sure this isn't what the author intended, but it's what her message implied.

While neurologists are pioneering research in the area of neuroplasticity and learning that there are aspects of our thinking that can rewrite our brains (which is life-changing!), and I also believe in the transformative power of prayer, it is damaging to send this simplistic message to hurting parents who are venturing into a pregnancy after loss. There is no magic formula to fertility. You can't wish the baby into staying or wish your body into working. So instead, I'll simply implore you to invite Jesus into your pregnancy. I suspect you already know how much he loves your child; please remember he loves you too. He is present to help you navigate this minefield.

Let me encourage you to bring your fears, doubts, anxieties, and insecurities to the Lord (1 Pet. 5:7). Start (or continue) learning the discipline of taking your irrational or unhelpful thoughts captive (2 Cor. 10:5). Choose daily to surrender your trust to Jesus (Prov. 3:5). Acknowledge your vulnerability but then allow his strength to be perfected in your weakness (2 Cor. 12:9–10). Humbly accept his grace (James 4:6). Let him uphold you (Isa. 41:10). Cast your burdens on him (1 Pet. 5:7). Meditate on truth, learn centering prayer, or practice mindfulness by coloring or journaling or jogging. Get professional counseling if you need to.[1] Love and be

---

1. It's a myth to think we can "pray away" all forms of depression and anxiety. If you have been practicing the spiritual disciplines as a way to manage your emotional and mental health but feel you're still struggling, please see your doctor for assessment. She or he will help you discern whether or not you need further help in the form of a personalized mental health plan (such as talk therapy, exercise, or medication). It is very normal to need this kind of support after miscarriage and other personal trauma.

loved (1 John 4:19). Continue your grieving process while also taking deliberate steps to let your heart feel joy (Isa. 61:3). Allow yourself to feel gratitude for your new pregnancy while acknowledging that your loss still hurts (Lam. 3:19–22). Let hope anchor your soul (Heb. 6:19).

When you're considering trying again but feel afraid, dive deep. When you're pregnant again and feel anxious, dive deep. When life feels precarious and your faith feels slippery, dive deep.

I promise you'll see God's goodness if you look for it.

Appendix E

Caring for a Friend after Miscarriage

According to Dr. Erica Berman, "Research consistently finds that women who have experienced a miscarriage feel that the responses of friends and family minimize the significance of the event and are dissatisfied with the support they receive."[1] The fact that you've sought out this resource demonstrates your desire for your friend to have the support she needs. *Thank you for being a good friend.*

Thank you for putting aside your discomfort, your awkwardness, and your own sadness, and for being willing to lower your guard and put yourself in the vulnerable position of offering help to a grieving friend.

As someone who's been on both sides of the coin—needing care and offering care—I'm well aware of the tightrope you walk as you try to navigate doing and saying the "right" things. Unfortunately, there's no road map for this, and quite frankly, most of us feel incredibly clumsy. That's okay. Grief is complicated to begin with, and grief from an intangible loss can seem even more complicated. It's just hard.

I have some bad news: You actually *might* do or say the wrong thing. You're at risk of sounding dumb or unintentionally doing or saying something hurtful to your friend who's already in pain. Because everyone grieves differently, it's impossible for me to tell you exactly what your friend needs to experience or hear. A lot of us let this possibility hold us back from trying. We're afraid of saying the wrong thing, so we say nothing. We're afraid of doing something insensitive, or making her pain worse, so we do nothing. But that's not you; you're actively looking for ways to help.

And, thankfully, I've got good news too: There is no one right way to help someone who's grieving—there are a million. And you—*her friend*—are in the best position to know how to care for her because you can listen to her, follow her cues, and gently offer support as she (or he) is willing to receive it. You know her personality, the things that make her exhale, and the things that cause her to knuckle down or run for cover. You know what makes her smile and what fills her cup with joy. You know her favorite drink from Starbucks and the snack she likes best while curled up watching Netflix.

Please bear in mind that the form your friend's grief takes may surprise you; don't let that deter you from continuing to offer friendship. She needs you now, whether she's able to see it clearly or not. Thank you in advance for your patience and your freedom to forgive if she takes for granted the care you offer.

Most importantly, never underestimate the power you have to minister through simple kindness and connection. Whatever you can do to help create space for her to process her grief and know she is loved will most likely be welcome. (Sometimes this means covering the practical work of cooking or cleaning so she can do soul work.) It doesn't take much to help a family in crisis find the difference between grieving with despair and *grieving with hope* as they process the loss of their child within a caring, supportive community. Mostly it just takes your presence. But it also takes small acts of compassionate action.

Think of it like this: Your friend has just experienced birth and death all at once. The things you might offer a new mother in the haze of postpartum hormones (yes, your friend has these too) are the same things she needs. And the things you might offer a friend after she's buried a loved one—these are the things she also needs.

Your willingness and generosity to offer practical, emotional, and spiritual support during this most tender of times can fortify a friendship like nothing else. Thank you for wanting to help carry brokenhearted parents through their pain.

I hope the following suggestions help. Because they aren't universal, I encourage you to always *offer* rather than *insist upon* these demonstrations of support.

1. Don't be silent.

Your friend and her family need to know they aren't alone. They may (or may not) ask for space, but even if they do, consider reaching out in a noninvasive way. Send a handwritten note or drop off flowers. At minimum send a text or write an email. She may not answer the phone or return your text straightaway, but that doesn't mean it wasn't appreciated. *Don't be silent just because you feel awkward.* Say simple things like, "I'm sorry," or "I'm thinking of you." Even if you've reached out by text or email, make sure to say something again when you see her in person: "I'm still so sorry for your loss."

2. Be available to listen and talk . . . or not.

Your friend may want to talk it all out, or she might prefer instead to talk about her favorite *Friends* episode or the latest weird fashion trend. It doesn't matter! (Your presence and availability are what matters.) She may find comfort in hearing your own story of loss, or she may wish you'd quietly listen. If social cues aren't clear enough, simply ask. (And then don't take her answer personally.) Continue to gently make known your availability.

3. Give her permission to feel whatever she's feeling.

Your friend is likely experiencing a huge range of emotions right now. Reassure her there's no singular "right" way to grieve and gently steer her away from comparisons if you sense she's sizing up her grief against someone else's. Her pain is the worst pain in the world because it's *hers*. It's important she feels validated—she's grieving the loss of her baby, and her sorrow (or whatever she's feeling) is normal. Remind her there's grace for the process.

(Note: If you think your friend's behavior *isn't* normal, or suspect she might be suffering from depression or PTSD, then urge her to visit a doctor or call a helpline for professional advice. If she is hesitant, call a helpline yourself and ask for suggestions for how to encourage her to get the help she needs. Obviously, if she's suicidal, then stay with her and immediately access emergency services.)

4. Refrain from offering pat answers or religious clichés.

A grieving parent doesn't need to hear things like, "God will never give us more than we can handle," or "Now you have an angel in heaven," or "Everything happens for a reason," or "That baby was too special for earth," or "God gives and takes away," or pretty much *any* form of "There's a reason this happened—it must be for the best." (I could make a very long list here, but I think you get the point.) Take care that you *don't inadvertently minimize her pain* by telling her she can try again or using any "at least" statements (e.g., "At least you weren't far along," "At least you know you can get pregnant," "At least you have other children," "At least you are young and can try again"). These well-intended sentiments can be very damaging for a grieving parent. Don't compare the loss of her baby to the loss of a pet, no matter how much of a beloved family member your fur baby was. In fact, don't compare the loss of her baby to any loss. Just let it be her own.

5. Offer practical help.

Women who have just lost babies often feel emotionally and physically exhausted, like *train wreck* exhausted. Some days she needs all her strength just to make it out of bed, so extra help with household chores and tasks can minister deeply. *An important tip: Don't make general offers such as "Let me know if you need anything."* When you're grieving, it's hard to make good on vague offers and articulate when you need the help. Take the guesswork out of things for her and offer something concrete instead: "I have a dinner planned for you; would Tuesday be okay to drop it by?" or "I have set aside some time to clean your bathroom and run a load of laundry; may I come later today, or would tomorrow be better?" (It's also worth noting again that you must follow her lead. Some women want to be left alone and would feel humiliated by someone coming to sweep up their hair-littered bathroom floor. If you can't figure out what she wants/needs, then ask her husband or ask her outright. Don't take it personally if she rejects your offer, but do offer again in a week or two.)

6. Don't assume someone else is looking after them.

Be mindful not to miss an opportunity to support a family after a loss because you think it's already covered by someone else. They need you now more than ever. I don't know a single woman who had "too much" support after a loss, but I sure do know a lot who felt they had too little.

7. If you are a person of faith, pray.

In addition to praying privately, consider offering to pray for the mother and father in person when you see them during a visit, at church, and so forth, or pray for them out loud over the phone. You could even type your prayer and send it in an email if you are uncomfortable praying aloud. Pray for her heart, her marriage, and her connection to Jesus. Don't fall victim to the "it's *just* prayer" mentality. Prayer is powerful, encouraging, and transformative. It is one of the greatest gifts you can offer to your friend.

8. Don't forget Dad.

Men experience grief and loss after a miscarriage too. In addition to the expectation that he's not to miss work, he's likely supporting his wife emotionally, assisting her practically as her body recovers, caring for other children, maintaining the home, and so on. He might seem to be holding it all together as he strives to maintain the status quo for the sake of his family, but *he's grieving too*. Ask yourself if there are small ways you can ease Dad's load, validate his pain, or demonstrate your support to him in a personal way. Include his name in cards you write and texts you send. Pray for him. Encourage him. Affirm him. Make room for his grief—welcome it, in fact.

9. Try to understand her triggers.

There's no way to know what capacity your friend will have to be around pregnant mothers and babies, but you can anticipate some of these sensitivities and gently ask her: "Does saying 'yes' to attend this baby shower feel like too much for you right now?" or "Would you rather not do the girls' night out, since many of the women going are new moms likely to be talking about baby milestones?" and so forth. Your friend may struggle with certain songs at church, holidays, family gatherings, or when a stranger asks how many kids she has. She may seem fine holding a friend's newborn one week and then months later, near her due date, not be able to bear the sight of fresh little babies even from a distance. No one assumes you have superpowers to read your friend's mind, but she'll appreciate you taking initiative to ask if certain things are hard for her; this gives her an opening to be honest, even when she worries what others will think. If nothing else, she'll appreciate your sensitivity and your willingness to try to understand.

10. Call her child by name.

If your friend has chosen a name for her baby, use it in cards, texts, and conversation. Hearing her baby's name spoken aloud helps give identity to her baby and validation to her grief.

11. Engage with her story.

If she's been vulnerable enough to share her story on social media or in a blog post, it's because she's hoping you'll read and engage with it, so please do. Rather than simply "liking" a post (which anyone can do), make a thoughtful comment or send a message letting her know you've read it. Thank her for being vulnerable. Tell her that her story and her baby's life matter. These are simple ways to validate her grief and show empathy.

12. Give her a thoughtful gift.

Put together a care package or buy her a thoughtful gift. (If you need specific ideas, I have a list on my blog—please see appendix F for the link.)

13. Mark your calendar.

Note anniversaries or other important days: what would have been the baby's due date, the date they received a horrible prognosis, the date of the miscarriage, or other significant dates such as Mother's Day or Father's Day. As those dates approach, do something small (even a text!) to remind her she's not alone. Knowing her baby and her grief are not forgotten will be a special comfort during those "marker" dates.

14. Be sensitive about "trying again" and future pregnancies.

Use discretion when enquiring about things like when they might try again, how many children they'd like to have, and so forth. Please understand that even if they do get pregnant again and carry a child to term, it will never replace the baby they lost. It's easy to think a new pregnancy will swap joy for their grief (and for some it does), but new pregnancies can also cause women to experience their grief all over again. Bear in mind that each woman handles this differently. If she gets pregnant again, she's likely to need extra support during her pregnancy as she copes with fear, anxiety, or other forms of grief.

Note: If you would like to email these suggestions to friends and family, you can download a PDF version at www.adrielbooker .com/miscarriage-stories-resources.

Appendix F

Resources and Support

The following resources are available at www.adrielbooker.com /miscarriage-stories-resources.

For Moms

What to expect physically when you miscarry

Mental health after miscarriage and loss

Body image after miscarriage and loss

Grief support forums

Stories of miscarriage, stillbirth, infertility, and other forms of loss

Pregnancy after loss

For Dads

Men and miscarriage

Grief support for dads

Stories from bereaved fathers

For Couples

Miscarriage and marriage

Sex and intimacy after miscarriage and loss

Communication after miscarriage and loss

For Children

How to help children process grief at different developmental ages and stages

Children's picture books on loss and grief

For Friends and Family

What to say (and not say) to someone who's lost a baby

How to support a friend through miscarriage (downloadable PDF)

Gift ideas for creating a care package

How to help a hurting mom on Mother's Day

Miscarriage and pregnancy/infant loss bereavement cards

For Care Providers

How your bedside manner and language can help a hurting parent after miscarriage

Spiritual Support

Scriptures for study and meditation after miscarriage and loss

Playlist of songs for grief and hope

Bible studies on grief and loss

Recommended books on the character of God, God's role in suffering, and heaven

Community

Our Scarlett Stories: An online community for parents who've lost babies to miscarriage and other forms of pregnancy and infant loss

Notes

Introduction

1. Colossians 3:3.

Chapter 1 Among the Fields of Gold

1. Matthew 6:9–10 ESV.
2. Psalm 34:8.
3. Colossians 1:17.

Chapter 2 Hello, Deep Dive

1. Richard Rohr, "Grieving as a Sacred Space," *Sojourners*, February 2002, https://sojo.net/magazine/january-february-2002/grieving-sacred-space.
2. Richard Rohr, "Liminal Space," *Richard Rohr's Daily Meditation*, July 7, 2016, http://myemail.constantcontact.com/Richard-Rohr-s-Meditation--Liminal-Space.html?soid=1103098668616&aid=jd48qU30R0U.

Chapter 3 The Spectacle of Heaven

1. C. S. Lewis, *The Complete C. S. Lewis Signature Classics* (Grand Rapids: Zondervan, 2002), 445.
2. Jemar Tisby, "Why My Grief Belongs on the Internet," *Christianity Today*, January 2016, http://www.christianitytoday.com/ct/2016/january-web-only/why-my-grief-belongs-on-internet.html.
3. Soong-Chan Rah, *Prophetic Lament: A Call for Justice in Troubled Times* (Downers Grove, IL: InterVarsity, 2015), 21–22.
4. One of the most radical examples of this in scripture is when Joseph is sold into slavery by his brothers and then eventually promoted to the highest position

under Pharaoh, where he's able to liberate his family from hunger and deliver them from certain calamity. See Genesis 37, 39–50, especially 50:20.

    5. Genesis 1:1.

    6. John 8:1–11; Luke 19:1–10; John 18:10; Acts 9:1–20; Luke 23:40–43; John 4:46–50; Luke 5:12–13.

    7. Mark 2:1–11.

Chapter 4 From the Dust

    1. *Strong's Concordance* 7210, *roi*, http://biblehub.com/hebrew/7210.htm.

    2. Henri Nouwen, *The Wounded Healer: Ministry in Contemporary Society* (New York: Doubleday, 1998), 72.

    3. John 1:1–5.

    4. John 1:14 MSG.

    5. John 1:1–5.

    6. John 1:17.

    7. *Strong's Concordance* 1145, *dakrýō* (from 1144 *dákry*, "tear-drop")—properly, to shed quiet (actual) tears; to weep silently (with tears), http://biblehub.com/greek/1145.htm.

    8. *Strong's Concordance* 2424, *Iēsoús*—Jesus, the transliteration of Hebrew term 3091, *Lôt* (*Yehoshua*/*Jehoshua*, contracted to *Joshua*), which means "*Yahweh* saves" (or "*Yahweh* is salvation"), http://biblehub.com/greek/2424.htm.

    9. The lion and lamb metaphors are used for Jesus throughout scripture, most notably in Genesis 49 (lion), Revelation 5 (lion and lamb), and John 1:29 (lamb).

    10. *Strong's Concordance* 2799, *klaiō*—properly, to weep aloud, expressing uncontainable, audible grief, http://biblehub.com/greek/2799.htm.

    11. John 11:32–35.

    12. "National Moral Revival Poor People's Campaign Watch Night Service, Valerie Kaur," Facebook video, 6:19, posted by Groundswell Movement on January 20, 2017, https://www.facebook.com/GroundswellMovement/videos/13280 29797267245/.

    13. *Merriam-Webster*, s.v., "compassion," https://www.merriam-webster.com/dictionary/compassion.

    14. Matthew 15:32.

    15. Matthew 20:34.

    16. Matthew 9:26.

    17. Mark 9:20–27.

    18. Luke 15:20.

    19. Matthew 18:27.

    20. *Strong's Concordance* 4697, *splagchnizomai*, http://biblehub.com/greek/4697.htm.

    21. Hebrews 1:3; John 14:6–11.

    22. Isaiah 55:8–9.

    23. Romans 8:35, 39.

    24. John 16:33.

    25. James 1:2–5.

26. 1 Peter 5:10. Peter is referring here to the suffering early Christians were enduring for their faith, yet I believe the promise for restoration applies for other ways of suffering too. See Revelation 21:4.

27. 1 Corinthians 2:9.

28. 2 Corinthians 12:9.

Chapter 5 Diary of a Broken Heart

1. C. S. Lewis, *A Grief Observed* (New York: HarperCollins, 2009), Kindle loc. 246.

2. Greg and Michele Russinger lead Portland Foursquare Church in Portland, Oregon, with this concept at its core—known by its congregants as Sideways PDX.

3. Patrick O'Malley, "Getting Grief Right," *New York Times Opinionator* (blog), January 11, 2015, http://opinionator.blogs.nytimes.com/2015/01/10/gett ing-grief-right.

Chapter 6 A Thousand Shades of Grief

1. Adriel Booker, *Miscarriage, Loss, and Faith Survey*, posted via Facebook, 756 responses, July 8, 2016.

2. Americans would call this a camping trailer.

3. 1 Samuel 1.

4. If you are new to liturgical prayer or would like to discover more, I recommend starting with *Common Prayer: A Liturgy for Ordinary Radicals* by Shane Claiborne.

5. Romans 8:26–27.

6. *Strong's Concordance* 4903, *sunergeó*, http://biblehub.com/greek/4903.htm.

Chapter 7 The Eighteen-Inch Journey

1. Curt Thompson, "How Neuroscience—and the Bible—Help Us Explain Shame," interview by Rob Moll, *Christianity Today*, June 23, 2016, http://www.christianitytoday.com/ct/2016/julaug/how-neuroscience-and-bible-explain-shame.html.

2. "The Power of Vulnerability | Brene Brown," YouTube video, 20:49, posted by TED on January 3, 2011, https://youtu.be/iCvmsMzlF7o.

3. Hebrews 4:16.

4. Genesis 2:25.

5. Genesis 3:7–10.

6. Genesis 3:21.

7. Thompson, "How Neuroscience—and the Bible—Help Us Explain Shame."

8. 1 John 4:8, 16.

9. "Listening to Shame | Brene Brown," YouTube video, 20:28, posted by TED on March 16, 2012, https://youtu.be/psN1DORYYV0.

10. Revelation 12:3.

11. Romans 5:8.

12. Ephesians 2:10.

13. Colossians 3:3.

14. Romans 8:35–39.
15. Revelation 21:4.
16. Romans 8:31.
17. 1 John 3:16.
18. Learn more about the Helser family's ministry at http://www.aplacefor theheart.org.

Chapter 8 An Invitation to Liberation

1. Romans 2:4.
2. Romans 2:4.

Chapter 9 Thistle Cove

1. Romans 12:15.
2. YWAM is an acronym for Youth With A Mission.
3. 1 John 4:8; Colossians 3:3.
4. John 3:16.
5. 2 Corinthians 5:18.

Chapter 10 A Crisis of Faith or a Catalyst for Grace?

1. Mark 4:35–41.
2. Hebrews 4:16.
3. See also John 1:1; John 14:9; Hebrews 1:3.
4. John 11:1–44.
5. *Strong's Concordance* 714, *arkeó*, http://biblehub.com/greek/714.htm.

Chapter 11 Whose Fault Is This, Anyway?

1. Naomi means "pleasant," while Mara means "bitter."
2. John 10:10.
3. Romans 2:4.
4. Matthew 7:9.
5. John 3:16.
6. Luke 13:34.
7. James 4:6.
8. Revelation 21:1–4.
9. A. W. Tozer, *The Knowledge of the Holy* (Grand Rapids: Zondervan, 1978), 1.
10. Luke 23:46.

Chapter 12 The Business of Tear-Wiping

1. C. S. Lewis, *The Last Battle*, The Chronicles of Narnia, vol. 7 (Glasgow, Scotland: Collins, 2001), 760.
2. Revelation 21:3.

3. *Strong's Concordance* 3824, *paliggenesía*, http://biblehub.com/greek/3824 .htm.

4. Jesus is recorded as referring to the "kingdom of heaven" in the Gospel of Matthew and the "kingdom of God" in the other Gospels.

5. Philippians 3:20.

6. Ecclesiastes 3:11.

7. Hebrews 13:14.

8. 2 Corinthians 5:17; Galatians 6:15; Ephesians 4:24.

9. *Strong's Concordance* 2537, *kainos*, http://biblehub.com/str/greek/2537.htm.

10. For further study on biblical eschatology and the renewal of all things, I recommend *Surprised by Hope* by N. T. Wright; *Futureville* by Skye Jethani; and *A New Heaven and a New Earth* by J. Richard Middleton.

11. Skye Jethani, *Futureville* (Nashville: Thomas Nelson, 2013), Kindle loc. 1093.

12. Jennifer Dukes Lee, "Out with the Pain, in with the Spirit (a Way to Breathe When Life Is Too Much)," *Jennifer Dukes Lee* (blog), September 12, 2017, http://jenniferdukeslee.com/pain-spirit-way-breathe-life-much/.

13. Revelation 21:1–4.

14. John 10:10.

Chapter 13 And Then She Laughed

1. Matthew 19:14.

2. Exodus 2:1–10.

3. Matthew 5:14 ESV; Matthew 5:3–10.

4. Sally Lloyd-Jones, *The Jesus Storybook Bible* (Grand Rapids: Zondervan, 2009), 210.

5. Revelation 12:11.

6. Jerry Sittser, *A Grace Disguised: How the Soul Grows through Loss* (Grand Rapids: Zondervan, 2009), 46.

Appendix C Helping Your Child Process Grief after Miscarriage

1. Child Mind Institute, "Helping Children Cope with Grief," accessed June 19, 2017, https://childmind.org/guide/helping-children-cope-grief/what-to-say -and-how-to-say-it/.

2. ChildGrief.org, "Navigating Children's Grief: How to Help Following a Death," accessed June 19, 2017, http://childgrief.org/documents/HowtoHelp.pdf.

3. See *The Five Love Languages* by Gary Chapman or http://www.5lovelan guages.com.

4. Dorina Gilmore, "Ten Creative Ways to Honor a Loved One," *Dorina Lazo Gilmore* (blog), May 26, 2017, http://dorinagilmore.com/10-creative-ways-to -honor-a-loved-ones-memory-and-clean-out-the-garage/.

Appendix E Caring for a Friend after Miscarriage

1. Erica Berman, "No Matter When It Happens, Loss of a Pregnancy Can Be Devastating," *The Huffington Post*, July 18, 2012, http://www.huffingtonpost.com /erica-berman/miscarriage-_b_1680949.html.

Adriel Booker loves helping people engage with the goodness of God, discover who they are in light of him, and find a sense of purpose where their gifts and passions collide with the needs of the world. She's the founder of The Love A Mama Collective, a movement of women empowering women through safe birth initiatives in developing nations, and is the curator of Our Scarlett Stories, an online community of parents supporting one another through pregnancy loss.

Originally from the mountains of Oregon, USA, Adriel has served in global missions for nearly two decades as a speaker, Bible teacher, writer, advocate, leadership coach, and mentor. She and her Aussie husband, Ryan, with their three young "Aus-Merican" boys, now live in the heart of Sydney, Australia, where they're cultivating an inner-city YWAM community and discovering the deep joy of living in a city by the sea. She dreams of the day when Jesus makes all things new and when she can sleep in until 9:00 a.m. on a regular basis.

Connect with Adriel at her blog, www.adrielbooker.com, where she explores topics related to faith and everyday spirituality, missions, family and parenting, motherhood, and global women's issues.

MEET
ADRIEL BOOKER

ADRIELBOOKER.COM

@ADRIELBOOKER

Connect with

BakerBooks
Relevant. Intelligent. Engaging.

Sign up for announcements about
new and upcoming titles at

www.bakerbooks.com/signup

 ReadBakerBooks

ReadBakerBooks

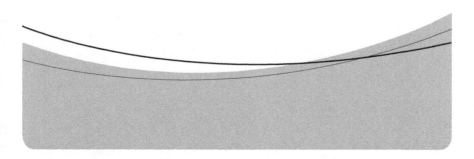

CPSIA information can be obtained
at www.ICGtesting.com
Printed in the USA
LVHW02s2047150518
577262LV00016B/1512/P

9 780801 075810